Peter Cornwell was ... the vicar of the Church of St Christopher, Brislington, on the outskirts of Bristol. Both sides of the family were connected with a dissenting tradition, but he was brought up in the middle stream of the Church of England.

His main schooling was at the Downs School in Wraxall and King's School, Bruton, both of which stimulated his life-long interest in politics – he became a Socialist and a Pacifist, which led him to become a conscientious objector. For his period of National Service Mr Cornwell joined the Friends' Ambulance International Service, and also joined the Transport and General Workers' Union.

After this he went to read theology at Worcester College, Oxford, completing his preparation for ordination at Cuddesdon Theological College. He was ordained to the diaconate of the Church of England in 1959 and to the priesthood the following year by the Archbishop of York, Michael Ramsey, as he was then working as a curate in North Hull. He returned to Cuddesdon to teach, and it was there that he met his future wife. In 1966 he became vicar of Silksworth, Co. Durham, in 1972 vicar of Barnard Castle, and then in 1975 vicar of the University Church of St Mary the Virgin, Oxford. He resigned that living in May 1985 and now lives in Hailey with his wife and two children.

PETER CORNWELL

One Step Enough

The Story of a Journey

Keep thou my feet; I do not ask to see
The distant scene; one step enough for me.

John Henry Newman

Collins
FOUNT PAPERBACKS

First published by Fount Paperbacks, London in 1986

Made and printed in Great Britain by
William Collins Sons & Co. Ltd, Glasgow

With love and gratitude to the Church of England and especially to those members of it who sustain me on my journey, Hilary, James and Elizabeth

Contents

Introduction   9

1. Childhood and School   13
2. Learning of Various Kinds   26
3. Ordination and Marriage   40
4. Silksworth and Chadwick   54
5. Barnard Castle   69
6. Oxford   92
7. "In you we have found a home"   119

Appendix   138

Introduction

When, on 19 May 1985, I told the congregation of the University Church of St Mary the Virgin in Oxford that I was about to become a Roman Catholic, I produced a brief, but carefully prepared, statement (see Appendix). That, at the time, seemed sufficient explanation and – knowing the perils of off-the-cuff comment and how such things could be twisted and bent to suit the requirements of a game of ecclesiastical cowboys and indians – to the probings of newspaper reporters I played a dead bat. Yet some friends remained puzzled by my move and said that more explanation was called for. So here it is. However I am aware that such "apologies" are a bit of a self-indulgence, and I have to admit that I have written as much for myself as for any who may want to listen in.

I find myself wrestling to reconcile two convictions, one that "to live is to change", that life really is a journey with the possibility of movement, and the other that the past always remains part of us, that it is perilous to neglect our "roots". But I am encouraged to share with others the fruit of this wrestling because fitting together these two convictions is more than a personal task; in its application to the institutions of divided Christendom it is part of what ecumenical work is about. If Churches remain stuck in the mud of their past and are unable to move, there will be no unity, and if Churches neglect their roots and the hand of God in their past, while there may be take-over bids, there cannot be that catholic unity which looks to the fulfilment, the gathering up of the riches, of our divided past.

> Lead kindly light . . .
> The night is dark and I am far from home
> Lead thou me on.

For Newman life was a journey in which the pilgrim, although he does not "ask to see the distant scene", prays that God will "keep" his feet so that the next step can be discerned. There are those for whom loyalty to roots is everything and who, knowing my Anglican background, have said that I could be nothing else. Now, although I admit that my past is obstinately part of me, I cannot admit that I am chained by that past for that would surely imply that there can be no change, no "conversions" at all. Yet all around us we see such changes taking place, individuals claiming the freedom to move out of their past. We may smile at the "fall and rise" of the Reginald Perrins of this world, the man of the city who throws away his bowler hat and umbrella and takes to being a crofter in the Outer Hebrides. Such dramatic changes can be dismissed as the outcome of a "mid-life crisis". But that, in itself, explains nothing. We know solid members of one political party who have switched their allegiance to another. We have even known those, brought up in the respectable conformity of atheist or agnostic homes, who become believers in God. If we are not free to change our past, we are nevertheless free to strike out into the future. So this is the story of one who has tried to be aware of all the forces which have shaped and fashioned him, but who has dared to believe that he has a real freedom to move. I have tried to follow conscience, holding this to be an absolute duty. In the weeks before I became a Roman Catholic, I read the Master of Balliol's delightful book *A Path from Rome*. As will be seen, I was not deterred in my course but I recognized in Tony Kenny a fellow pilgrim. We might seem to be going in opposite directions but we were both trying to follow where we believed the argument was leading us. To invoke "conscience" is not to opt out of rationality, to claim some sort of devine flash of illumination which makes argumentation unnecessary, but to make sure that conscience is well-informed, that pros and cons are properly weighed. "Conversion" is not a happy word to describe the step I have taken as, strictly speaking, one can only be converted to God, and so modern Roman Catholics are rightly reluctant to use this word of an individual's return to catholic unity. What one prays though is that this movement is one step in the life-long process of being converted to God. It is but one step and not journey's end. That will come when we no longer see through a glass darkly but face to face.

If our freedom to take faltering steps is real, it matters that we move with a great love for our past, reconciled with our roots. Quite clearly there are those for whom this has not happened who, changing direction, feel obliged to reject and even despise their past. In recent years we have met those who have been "converted" from the pale political pink of their youth to the bright blue of Conservatism and, as twice-born monetarists, they are sometimes to be heard mocking the idealism and naïvety of their youth. We have known ex-Methodists and ex-Anglicans who have felt compelled to speak scornfully of those Christian communities in which God has fed and led them. Such rejection of the past is not only unlovely and ungrateful but can store up trouble for the future. Precisely because that past cannot be destroyed it may behave with all the viciousness of an unrequited lover. I have known Jews whose families have cut their moorings and drifted into Christianity, who suddenly awake to the tug of their Judaistic roots and long to reclaim them. There is real agony in the question, "Can I be a Christian and still remain a Jew?" I find myself echoing this dilemma in the question, "Can I be a Roman Catholic and still be an Anglican?" The sadness of Newman's life as a Catholic was, not so much that his gifts were not used, but that he found it so difficult to be that Anglican Roman Catholic he inescapably was. The doors were not quite wide enough open to receive some of the treasures he had to bring into Catholic unity. And yet in his poem Newman looks forward to the joy of rediscovering what had been so precious in his past:

> And with the morn those angel faces smile
> Which I have loved long since and lost a while.

I doubt whether those who have asked for further explanation will be satisfied. Explanations of this sort are about as successful as explanations of why one has married this girl and not that. You may describe her eyes, her hair, her smile, the warmth of her character but, to the outsider, it will still all be a great mystery. If explanations fail, the exercise of putting pen to paper will still be justified if I emerge from the task a bit more thankful for my past and a bit more convinced that this one step has led to the fulfilment of what was precious in that past.

ONE

Childhood and School

The journey began in 1934 when, in the Church of St Christopher, Brislington, of which my father was the vicar, I was baptized by my godfather, Clifford Salisbury Woodward, then Bishop of Bristol. Although both sides of the family connect with a dissenting tradition, my own roots were firmly Anglican, as great-grandparents had moved to occupy the evangelical wing of the Church of England. It was not an inflexible position; my mother's mother had been sent to the convent school at Wantage and retained a life-long respect for the nuns who had taught her. In 1936, on my father becoming rector of St Paul's, Chippenham, we moved from a Bristol suburb to the life of a Wiltshire market town. Here we were brought up in what would then have been considered the middle stream of the Church of England. It was the religion of mattins, afternoon Sunday School, and daily family prayers, a religion based on the Bible, the Prayer Book and *Hymns Ancient and Modern*, in liturgical tone "low church" rather than excitedly evangelical, a religion of gentle growth rather than of challenge and sudden conversion. It was not overtly much interested in sacraments. On certain Sundays our elders stayed behind after the Morning Service for the midday celebration of Holy Communion, an event clothed in as much mystery as sex. Children, if not excluded, were not expected to attend.

My father, a committed parish priest, was a careful preacher whose Bible was methodically annotated to show exactly where and when each sermon had been preached. At times he would check through this Bible to make sure that his congregation was receiving a balanced diet. I can recall him looking up from such a perusal to say: "I have not preached on the Book of Esther for many years. It is time I did." Such carefully balanced expository preaching saved his congregation from the boredom of being continually bombarded by the clergyman's over exercised hobby horses, and always came alive, as it was married to pastoral experience and wisdom acquired through diligent parochial visiting. Indeed, Father threw himself into the full range of a parish priest's activity; he was never fastidious or complaining about necessary administrative chores but performed them all with meticulous care, whether it was mowing the rectory lawn in preparation for a missionary garden party or installing, with the help of his sons, a gigantic Christmas tree in the church. All such operations were performed with military precision.

Life was not all a church-centred nurture of the faithful. Father was a true parish priest and never the chaplain of an enclosed sect. He thus sank into the soil of his particular patch of the Lord's Vineyard, became involved in it and fascinated by all, whether sacred or secular, that went on in it. He had a genuine interest and respect for the expertise of others, and would listen with fascination to the station master or the builder talking about his work. God, it was made clear to us, could not be confined to the world of ecclesiastical activity. This was reinforced by my mother, who had a decent impatience with what she called "churchiness" and, when father became an archdeacon, she was quite unimpressed by all those committees he sat on, in her heart of hearts believing that this world of ecclesiastical administration was of dubious value. For Mother, the most uninstitutional of Christians, the local and individual alone mattered. Her remarkably loving heart sought out and seemed to find something good in everyone. If the archdeacon passed judgement on some erring or incompetent clergyman, Mother could be relied upon to act as counsel for the defence. Her faith was simple and practical; impressive ceremonies or cascades of fine-sounding words were to her but sounding brass and tinkling cymbals unless cashed in terms of love. This motherly warmth, combined with father's necessary touch of steel, fashioned for their four sons a framework of remarkable stability. We knew that, whatever we did or did not do, we would still be held in that love. Nor was the caring claustrophobic, locked up in the family circle. Ours was an open house, and throughout the war we welcomed into the home servicemen from every quarter of the globe. If there was a household rule it was that we were expected to show courtesy and respect for each individual; only contempt or snobbery would earn from Mother a rare outburst of wrath.

This gentle mid-stream Anglicanism is often dismissed as charming but superficial. The busy mockers underestimate it. Grandmother Rudman, who lived with us in her latter days, revealed something of the depth of this tradition. Like many of her generation, she was a monthly communicant, but we could not fail to be impressed by the care with which she prepared for these great occasions. Her spirituality was fed by the Bible, Bunyan's *Pilgrim's Progress* and *The Imitation of Christ*. In her we glimpsed that solid rock which must lie at the heart of all genuine loving, and there was communicated to us something of the seriousness of God. Her preparation for death made a tremendous impression. During her last months, she busied herself labelling all her possessions, so that it should quite clearly be known to whom each item was to go, and then she settled back in bed to plan, with similar care, the details of her own funeral. Nowadays, with the business of dying pushed away into hospitals, the young are deprived of such examples of a free and dignified handing back to God of the life he has given.

All this was a very distinctive Church of England world,

and yet in it we experienced the growing longing for Christian unity. My father always treated Nonconformist ministers as equals and colleagues, and was a keen member of the local fraternal where ministers would meet for prayer, Bible study and discussion. Of Roman Catholics we knew little or nothing. On the way to the railway station, we would pass the red-brick R.C. church but had little interest in what might be going on inside. Catholics, we were led to believe, kept themselves to themselves and imagined that they alone were heading for heaven. In fact my father's brother was a Roman Catholic, but that was considered understandable as he had married a Belgian girl and, after the war, returned to Belgium as a bank manager. It was all right for foreigners to be R.C.

I am grateful for this central Anglican tradition, which cut through the complexities of religion and sent us straight to the heart of the matter. It was a religion of Jesus of Nazareth, of the stories about him, and of our joy in both retelling "the old, old story" and trying to follow in his footsteps. "Is this action or that Christlike?" we were taught to ask. This was the religion of 1 Corinthians 13, with its insistence that, in the end, all will pass away save love. This was the religion of the First Epistle of St John: "Everyone that loveth is born of God and knoweth God." Although I was to come to believe that the "unsearchable riches of Christ" required a more all-embracing and fuller articulation, yet I have also come to recognize the need for a continued return from "riches" back to this simplicity, for without this coming back to the basic thing, we fail to see the wood for the trees, and the riches, far from mediating the riches of Christ, begin to clutter and mask his face. I am not the tidiest of people and my study easily slips into chaos, but a moment comes when I know this is intolerable and that the clutter must be cleared away to recapture the space in which alone I can work.

Such clearing of space, the activity of pur▬
be part of the rhythm of faith.

I never felt the religion of my childhood a▬
burden. I do not recall there being much fuss▬
about getting us children to church. It was ▬
those things, like helping with the washing up or doing
errands, which members of the family did. Of course there
was much boredom as we wended the somewhat pon-
derous way through full choral mattins, a boredom which,
if unrelieved by eyecatching ceremonial, could be
alleviated by studying the eccentricities of those in neighbouring pews or the antics of choirboys. I think that the
only point where the shoe pinched was over the question
of Sunday observance. My father had been quite a strict
Sabbatarian and my grandmother was a paid up member
of the Lord's Day Observance Society. Sunday cricket in
the garden was frowned upon, and an attempt was made
to lure us into suitable games which got round the Sabbath
prohibition by the introduction of biblical characters. Substitute Mr Jesse the Sheepfarmer for Mr Bung the Brewer
and you could have Happy Families fit for Sunday. But,
by and large, religion was for us a broad room in which
we were encouraged to move around, ask questions and
discuss issues.

My initial experience of school was a dismal failure.
This was partly due to almost continuous severe earache,
which eventually resulted in an operation, but mainly to
my entry into a preparatory school which purveyed a hard
evangelical line. I quite enjoyed learning to make a model
Palestinian lamp in the Crusaders, and did not even rebel
against the headmaster's wife teaching us to recite the
hymn "Every morning the red sun riseth warm and
bright", but I could not stand her husband, who ruled over
us, cane in one hand and Bible in the other. It was my first
taste of a religion of fear, and I fled from it into the com-
parative comfort of being ill. Wisely my parents swiftly

...sferred me to the more informal world of the Downs School at Wraxall, thus following in the footsteps, not only of my elder brother, but, as I later discovered, of Mervyn Stockwood. The Downs School, in my day, was presided over by Aelfric Harrison, a wily left-arm bowler and Latin enthusiast. Here I was back again in gentler religious pastures. Aelfric Harrison could be severe and his left arm adept at exercises other than bowling, but at least he did not mix up discipline with piety. The religious framework was sober and quite without excessive zeal, and every Sunday morning we had to learn the collect for the day, which had to be recited to the headmaster before we were marched the considerable distance to Wraxall parish church for morning prayer, conducted by an elderly and nicely eccentric clergyman. It was at the Downs School that I had my first encounter with a religion other than low church. A friend, who like me suffered the agonies of homesickness, used to turn to a rosary for consolation.

But, if school failed to fire my religious enthusiasm, it was the place of my conversion to politics. My grandmother was a staunch Tory and she used to get me to send a Christmas card each year to our local M.P., Mr David, now Lord, Eccles. This Conservative allegiance was fed by a book which I discovered in the school library, giving a lurid description of the Russian Revolution. At this time a new member of the staff boldly announced that she was a Communist. Stirred with indignation, I identified her with all the excesses of Lenin, and felt it a matter of principle to spit discreetly whenever she passed by. One day she spotted me indulging my protest and firmly slapped my face. It was my first experience of martyrdom. Yet I became fascinated by the whole mechanics of politics, and spent hours, with a dice, playing lone games of General Elections. An end of term song, made up to include the foibles of every boy and staff member, had the line:

"Cornwell runs General Elections for fun." It was at the Downs School that I was to hear the result of the 1945 General Election. Coming at the end of the term, I should have been full of elation, but instead, I am told, I appeared at breakfast ashen-faced at the fall of Winston Churchill.

At King's School, Bruton, both religion and politics took a somewhat different turn. Geoffrey Sale, the headmaster, was a solid middle of the road Anglican who combined a deep spirituality with a rich humanism. Every Sunday morning he was seen kneeling at the early celebration of Holy Communion. He was evidently a man of prayer yet his piety embraced all that he did, whether he was refereeing his much loved rugby or was with zest producing school plays. I suppose that he did not have quite the organizational and advertising skills which seem looked for in headmasters these days, but, to one schoolboy who hated the raw world of school, Geoffrey Sale stood for decent and humane values. I do not suppose he ever realized how much he taught us by the faith and courage he showed when his beloved wife died of cancer. When I arrived at the school it was still suffering from the wartime shortage of competent teachers, and I cannot say that I was initially inspired with much fervour for learning. However, by the time I reached the Sixth Form, two young men, straight from university, not only introduced me to the excitements of History and English Literature but also managed to instil in me some intellectual disciplines. I began to learn that wild ideas had to be built on a careful accumulation of evidence.

At Bruton my faith developed and I became sure of a vocation to the ministry of the Church. In all this the chaplain, Kenneth Ashcroft, played a significant part. Combining his duties with those of the vicar of a nearby village, he was able to have one foot in a camp not absorbed by school life. This was a great advantage, for schools can become intense and suffocating communities, and K.A., standing somewhat on the touchlines, was able to give us a sense of proportion by his irreverent mockery of some of those things, such as games and the Combined Cadet Corps, which were taken too solemnly. He was creatively subversive. His religion was of a flamboyant Anglo-Catholic variety, but it was not all frills and fancies; he had grand tales to tell of priests like Conrad Noel who combined ritualism with socialism and, in his divinity lessons, took us somewhat deeper than the normal diet of the travels of St Paul, to the arguments of Thomas Aquinas for the existence of God. Too often the teaching of divinity makes religion trivial; Kenneth Ashcroft tried to show us it was worthy of our respectful intellectual attention. About this time Geoffrey Sale began to invite to the school the Anglican Franciscan brothers from Hillfield in Dorset. They made a considerable impact by showing us a faith, both evangelical and catholic, which managed to capture the imagination. Some members of staff were, I know, a little disturbed at this introduction of religious enthusiasm into the school.

As a result of all this, I became a sort of Anglo-Catholic; "sort of" I say because I could not quite buy the whole package. K.A. could have me on the edge of my seat talking about the goings-on of the Red Vicar of Thaxted, but my enthusiasm waned when he expounded Adrian Fortescue on the ritual niceties of the Roman rite. What now mattered for me was a thorough-going sacramental Christianity. I began to feel that the trouble with low church worship was that God seemed distanced from us, as if there were an almost deliberate attempt to keep the Almighty at arm's length. In later years, when I tried to ease high altars away from the far east walls, I met some quite passionate opposition. "I like my communion far off, Vicar", was the cry of one aggrieved parishioner. Sacramentalism embodied what seemed central to the

Christian faith: the mystery of God coming near, to be accessible to us flesh and blood creatures. Of course "mateyness" with God, God "my chum", is a very terrible thing; if God be God he has to be the one who takes my breath away, and all that witnesses to this by way of word, music or sign is of the greatest value, but the Gospel is to do with the coming near of precisely this Holy God, of the inaccessible one making himself accessible. This is what I saw expressed in sacramental religion. Here was no denial of my evangelical past but an enrichment of it. Jesus the living Lord had stepped out of the story and become tangible. To come to Holy Communion was to meet with the risen Jesus. To come to Confession was to hear his word spoken personally to me: "Son, be of good cheer; your sins are forgiven."

Thus I began to discover something of the comprehensive power of catholicism. Nothing positive in my past need be lost; all was gathered up and reaffirmed. So I have never ceased to believe in the Reformation battle cry "By Grace alone". My experience of sacramental Christianity has been simply of this fact that all our doings and searchings are overshadowed by the action and searching of God himself. Indeed I have to record that my conversion to a belief in justification by faith came, not as the result of some evangelistic rally, but through the Eucharist and the confessional. These were the places where I discovered the Cross, where the words of old hymns – "Nothing in my hands I bring, simply to thy Cross I cling", "Just as I am without one plea" – came alive. But, if I could continue to say a wholehearted "yes" to the positive affirmations of the Reformation, I became increasingly saddened by its negations. Why should these noble affirmations require a "no" to these very things which made the affirmations real to me? How sad it is that Anglican evangelicals still resist the inclusion of prayer for the dead, the recognition of the saints' prayer for us and a form for the sacrament of reconciliation, in the official service books of the Church of England. For ordinary Christians, with no axe to grind, prayer for the dead or the saints' prayer for us, granted the reality of Christ's resurrection, seem the most natural things in the world. What is prayer but our share in the strong, wise loving of God? We pray for the dead and believe they pray for us simply because we know that our "last enemy" has been defeated, and that death cannot destroy our mutual loving. As one who, in later years, was to sit through more Memorial Services than he would care to count, I am bound to say that a service which centres on a recital of the alleged merits of the departed, seems far less evangelical than does a Requiem Mass which looks firmly away to the saving merits of Christ crucified.

Alas, Anglo-Catholicism had its own negations – not least its cool attitude to the Nonconformist churches. I always thought that the fear of somehow allowing "the full faith" to be sullied by what was alleged to be error, showed a distinct lack of confidence in that "full faith". If the ark were as strong as it was claimed to be, then surely it need not be quite so anxiously guarded. In any case, if what we claimed in our "high" doctrine of baptism were true, then we should see that baptized Christians essentially belonged together. Separated we might be, but in fact we remained brothers and sisters, and the activity of ecumenism to overcome these unnatural separations was imperative.

Maybe of more significance for my understanding of Christian unity was my political conversion. The boy who had mourned the defeat of Churchill became a Socialist and Pacifist. The family insistence that every human being should be treated as of equal value was making itself felt. At school I encountered for the first time that irrational and destructive phenomenon, English class consciousness. Slighting references were made to local lads who did not enjoy the privileges of private education. Boys from a colonial background spoke without inhibition of "niggers", as of a lower race. All this seemed not only hateful but silly. How could the accident of birth, wealth or colour make some people more important than others? And yet this absurdity was deeply embedded in English society.

Socialism, I learned, proclaimed the equality of man, not in the sense that everyone was the same but as the perception that each individual is valuable, not because of wealth, ability or power but simply because he or she is a human being. If we were all equal in the eyes of God, then it was time we began to see things his way. It was a sort of gut perception. When I hear it said, even by ecclesiastics, that there are no moral absolutes, I find myself protesting that there are some things which hit us in the face with the force of being absolutely true. Such seems the insight into the equal value of persons. It is hard to deduce it from the evidence, for if you look to the outward show of virtue, ability or power, you will come up with a picture of hopeless inequality. Indeed it is in those extreme cases, whether of the severely mentally retarded or of the unborn child, that the doctrine of the equal value of persons is really challenged.

Yet once we give way and abrogate to ourselves the task of deciding that some are more equal than others, we slip into a bottomless pit of horror. Our age has seen all too much of the fate of disposable persons. Those who mock at moral naïvety and tell us that everything is far more complex than we imagine, need to beware of the danger of blunting that moral directness, without which civilization is in peril. Of course the application of such "simple truth" can be a highly complex matter, and I suppose that, when converted to a belief in equality, I as yet failed to see the careful steps which are needed to embody, however imperfectly, this simple compelling insight. The need for politics, in the sense of the search for the next faltering step in the right direction, was to be seen later; but it remains important, in the face of those who would blind us with complexity, to insist that in the affairs of the city of man there has to be a movement backwards and forwards between the fundamental vision and the mechanics of its embodiment. "Youthful idealism" retains its own insight, for it is no good plodding ever so carefully if we do not know the direction in which we should be going.

I suppose that it was the same insight into the value of persons which made me revolted by the horror of war and led me to pacifism. We were treating our fellow human beings as disposable things. Now boys at King's School, Bruton, were "expected" (public school jargon for compelled) to join the Combined Cadet Corps. This mainly involved a good deal of Dad's Army comedy such as being commanded one afternoon, on a wind-swept hill, "to dig imaginary slit trenches", but occasionally, equipped with rifles and Bren guns, we could not avoid seeing the object of it all; we were being taught to kill. Measured by the question I had been taught to ask, "What would Christ do?", the answer seemed clear. So I announced to the Commanding Officer and the headmaster that I would lay down my musket. The authorities were mildly thrown. "See what happens", some said, "when a school encourages religious enthusiasm!" I was, by then, quite senior and generally considered a responsible character. What was to be done? The chaplain could not get me to snap out of it for, truth to say, although he was no pacifist, he relished such signs of rebellion. In fact Geoffrey Sale and his colleagues handled the matter with such sympathy and care that I was given two lessons in one. I was taught something about the inevitability of having to make a moral stand, and about the strength of sane tolerance in the face of dissent. Such a wise humane exercise of authority, from which ecclesiastics could learn much, saved me from being just a wild-eyed, self-righteous, angry young man. Instead of being edged out onto the margins of the community I was allowed to remain reasonably normal, making some progress with my studies, appearing as the Prince of Wales in Henry IV Part I, and playing the cricket I loved so much. My little bit of nonconformity was held in a very conformist framework, and I found that this normality made my friends less ready to dismiss my views as mere madness.

So justice and peace were, from these early days, wedded to my longing for unity amongst Christians. Any idea that Christians seek to unite in order to gang up on the world plainly contradicts the gospel insistence that Jesus died to gather into one all the scattered children of God. We pray that his followers should be one so that the world can see a sign that, in our rich diversity, we really do belong together.

TWO

Learning of Various Kinds

As those were the days of National Service, on leaving school my convictions had to be put to the test. When the call-up papers arrived, I requested to be registered as a conscientious objector. This meant that I had to appear before a tribunal presided over by an elderly judge, who was on record as claiming that "loving your enemies" was an immoral and subversive injunction. However, nobly supported by witnesses who, whilst all disagreeing with my views, were willing to testify to their belief that they were "conscientiously" held, and treated, even by the ferocious judge, with complete fairness, I passed this ordeal. For alternative service I joined the Friends' Ambulance International Service, which gave me an experience at least as profitable as that enjoyed by my friends who went into the armed forces. After an initial period of training at headquarters in Wiltshire, learning to make concrete, cleaning lavatories, and making soup with scrapings of stale porridge in the kitchen, I was sent to work as an orderly in a geriatric hospital. In the 1950s such hospitals were the slums of the infant National Health Service; inhabiting bleak old workhouses, crowded and understaffed, the care given was lamentably basic. Although orderlies were meant to do only the most menial tasks, washing and feeding patients, taking them to the lavatory, making beds and laying out the dead, so short-staffed were we that a raw lad straight from school could find himself, on night duty, in charge of some sixty very sick and confused old men.

One night I wrestled with a patient who kept popping

out of bed, putting on his cloth cap, and setting off, night shirt flapping around his legs, for the races. All the while in neighbouring beds three other old men lay dying. After such a night, I used to find relief by nipping out of the ward to watch the new day dawning and enjoy a quiet smoke. The work was often dirty and depressing. Some old people can be quite delightful but others can be aggressive and demanding. One such, sustained by a daily bottle of Guinness and frequent nips of whisky, lived to the age of one hundred and five. Once, dispatched to give him a blanket bath, I had to make my advance to his bedside under a shower of empty Guinness bottles dispatched as an expression of his displeasure at such an indignity. God seemed to be testing my rather theoretical high-mindedness. Could I face up to the realities of the human situation, the angry, the resentful, the incontinent and the disturbed, and go on seeing the face of Christ looking out at me through the least of his brethren? The slender resources of my love were exposed, and I found myself driven back to the constant spring of divine love. I knew that I needed the grace of God as I had never needed it before. If love was tested so was faith. It is easy to believe in the goodness of God if you are beside the lake beneath the trees with daffodils dancing and fluttering in the breeze, or if you are enjoying the comforts of a warm and loving home, but when your position is shifted and you come face to face with the degradations of old age and with terminal illness, and when, during the course of one night, you have laid out three corpses, then the world looks more bleak, the sovereignty of goodness less likely. There were moments when I felt a sheer disgust and hatred for this monstrous burden of suffering around me.

Political idealism was tested as well, and I began to think seriously about the ways and means through which the equal value of persons could be affirmed. Of course the fire of love cannot be lit by institutions and political arrangements, but there are structures which can encourage or discourage the growth of a caring society. The National Health Service was a great advance, but it was clear that we needed to keep renewing our initial vision to save us from complacency and to keep us labouring to improve the machinery. Along with my fellow orderlies, I became a member of the Transport and General Workers' Union, and so was able to discover the many unadvertised ways in which trades unions find themselves working for causes other than wage bargaining. A good deal of pressure for improvement in the standards of our hospital came in fact from our tiny branch.

Membership of the Friends' Ambulance Unit inevitably brought me into contact with the religion of the Society of Friends. At headquarters every day began with a Quaker meeting, and I learned to appreciate this distinctive style of worship with its silent waiting on God, although I am bound to say that I found the silence more edifying than the occasions when individuals were moved to speak. Yet, while I was enthusiastic about the affirmations of the Quakers, their courageous stand for justice and peace and the particular dimensions of their worship, I found their negations, the rejection of creeds, sacraments and liturgical forms, a diminishment. Human beings are not angels, and need something to sign and symbol if the mystery of God is to touch them. As my hospital work left me weary and drained I knew my need of the grace of God mediated through the outward and visible. After all, our faith centres on the fact that out of his silence God has spoken and that word has been made flesh. It is this failure to make those concessions to the flesh which God himself has made, which makes the Society of Friends a very cerebral sort of community. While I have seen it flourishing amongst intellectuals and the spiritually sensitive, I have yet to discover its meeting houses in the inner city.

But it seemed to me that there was no need for these

denials. All that Quakers wanted to see affirmed could be affirmed within the context of a fuller and more balanced expression of Christianity. So once again I glimpsed the comprehensive power of catholicism, for while you could not be a Quaker and enjoy the benefits of creeds and sacraments, you could inhabit a more catholic form of Christianity and still take in the values of the Quakers. I was all for having the best of every world. This conviction was reinforced by my friendship with Kenneth and Elizabeth Clark. When my father became Archdeacon of Swindon, we moved from Chippenham to the straggling north Wiltshire village of Brinkworth. Here Kenneth, an ex-Baptist minister, became his curate and with his wife kept open house so that, on my visits home from hospital work, we would spend hours talking and laughing about everything under the sun. What impressed me about Kenneth was the total absence of anything like that "convert mentality" which seems to involve a harsh rejection and even despising of one's past. He remained deeply grateful for all that had been given him as a Baptist but had come to believe that this treasure needed to be held in a more comprehensive container. A thoroughly evangelical faith required catholic embodiment.

It was while working at the old people's hospital outside Bristol that I came into contact with the remarkable inner city parish of St Matthew Moorfields, which was then under the leadership of Mervyn Stockwood. This church brought together the disconnected threads of my concerns. It was evangelical, always concerned with a straightforward yet intelligent preaching of the Gospel, and catholic, with the centre of its life the Eucharist celebrated with considerable splendour. Indeed, with its smells and bells, St Matthew's could have been yet another Anglo-Catholic shrine, but here there was nothing exclusive or merely exotic, it looked firmly outwards from its eucharistic centre. It was in the forefront of ecumenical work involved in the pioneering venture of the Redfield United Front. It was also committed to the social needs of the area. Mervyn was, in those days, famous or notorious for his known membership of the Labour Party, and in fact was an elected City Councillor yet, although he insisted on the need for Christian political involvement, he never equated Christianity with Socialism. Those of other political persuasions never felt excluded from the church, and over the years there worshipped at St Matthew's, not only Sir Stafford Cripps, but also Sir Walter Monkton. I have heard a good many vintage Stockwood sermons and, while they were all masterly expositions of the faith which managed to capture the heart and the mind, none that I recall purveyed party politics. For articulating the inclusive powers of catholicism and welding together my ecumenical and political aspirations, I owe a great debt of gratitude to this little church. If I was on the late shift at the hospital, I would often rise early to catch the bus into the city and attend a midweek Eucharist at St Matthew's. If that suggests an excessive piety, I might add that the occasion was rounded off with the earthier delight of a leisurely reading of the *Guardian* over bacon and eggs at Temple Meads Station.

National Service completed, I went up to Worcester College, Oxford, to read theology, in the autumn of 1954. Like others who had experienced this enforced break in our education, I found Oxford somewhat petty. We who had learnt to take some responsibility found ourselves regressing into a world still designed for ex-schoolchildren. The rules at Worcester included one which required that gentlemen should attend chapel every Sunday. Unlike a later more revolutionary generation we were surprisingly submissive; perhaps our service in disciplined organizations had taught us the art of bending rather then confronting such rules. Packed into three swift eight-week terms, undergraduate life is intense and exhausting. There is so much to do that, in the natural desire not to miss out on anything, you are tempted to take on too much and then you are in danger of simply sinking under the weight of it all. I was able to pursue my love of the theatre with the Worcester College Buskins and appeared as Trinculo in *The Tempest* with Tim Bavin, the present Bishop of Portsmouth, as Ariel. My political interests were fed by membership of both the Labour Society and the further to the left Socialist Society, but as, apart from a few dedicated enthusiasts, we were not over solemn about our politics, we mainly joined these for the opportunity to hear famous speakers.

This willingness to attend meetings in order to sit at the feet of those who seemed to have something important to say spilled over into the sphere of religion. On a Saturday at dinner, undergraduates could be heard discussing which preacher they would hear the following day. Would it be the Archbishop of Canterbury at St Mary's, Austin Farrer at Pusey House, or the Bishop of Liverpool at St Ebbe's? While there was a solid core of committed Christians, there was a wider fringe of enquirers and fellow travellers who believed religion to be of some importance. Oxford presents the student with a bewildering à la carte menu of religious experience, with every nuance of Church of England life apparently represented – from the lowest St Ebbe's up a shade through St Aldate's to scale the heights of Pusey House or St Mary Magdalen's and even, in those days, through the roof to the papalist church of St Paul's in Walton Street.

All this is fascinating but encourages religious tasting rather than commitment, and I confess that, after St Matthew Moorfields, I found nothing really to my taste. There was always the University Church occupying a solid if rather dull middle. Its Sunday evening sermons were often a feast for the mind, but its careful avoidance of

31

liturgical extremity made for rather depressing worship. The heart was better served by the High Mass at Pusey House, but this I found a little precious. I failed to discover, until too late, the extraordinary personal ministry exercised by its Principal, Hugh Maycock, who, amidst endless cups of coffee and wrapped in clouds of cigarette smoke, gently led many in the ways of faith. For religious anchorage Worcester College Chapel became my base where the chaplain, Bobby Milburn, managed to provide a home for both the wildest Anglo-Catholic and the most hard line Evangelical. Bobby is a pre-Tractarian high churchman who, behind the somewhat eighteenth-century pursuit of decent moderation, embodies a deep but unostentatious piety. He was able to be all things to all men, not because he was indifferent, but because he could penetrate behind party labels to get to that one thing necessary which united us all.

Ecumenism in Oxford was spearheaded by the then flourishing Student Christian Movement. By never threatening the integrity or identity of the churches from which its members came, it was able to provide an admirable meeting place for Christians of all traditions. Indeed, it is interesting to notice that it flourished at the same time as did the separate denominational societies but that, when in an act of ecumenical fervour the latter committed suicide, the former also began to wither and fade. Whatever the unity of Christians means, it cannot be the setting up of some brand new Super-Church which requires that we cut our roots with the past. It was sad that we were deprived of Roman Catholic participation in these ecumenical ventures. Of course during Weeks of Prayer for Christian Unity there were notable contributions from Catholic speakers, yet on these occasions we were still slightly on edge awaiting the flash of steel of Roman intransigence, and you could not be quite sure that the Catholic speaker might not walk off the platform if some innocent chairman dared to break into prayer. This strongly defended city was undoubtedly effective for there were many "conversions" at that time, but it was a missed opportunity, for other Christians were genuinely longing to understand the Catholic position and to receive what it had to offer. We respected this solid chunk of rock and knew that there was something here we all needed but we could not receive it if it were simply hurled at us from outside. However, back in the more informal atmosphere of the College, Bobby Milburn seemed able to draw into our chapel discussion group a handful of highly intelligent and ecumenically sensitive Catholics. This helped us to glimpse what might be possible if only those tantalising locked doors could be opened.

The aim and object of the exercise at Oxford was, of course, to study theology. Bobby Milburn, my tutor as well as chaplain, was of the old school which resisted the farming out of pupils to a variety of experts. Perhaps we missed out on some of the stimulus and excitement derived from specialists, but there were solid advantages in sticking to our General Practitioner. "Do not read too many books" was Bobby's surprising advice to Tim Bavin and me and, as we saw our contemporaries weighed down with vast reading lists, we believed ourselves in receipt of a higher wisdom. Oxford teaching, like the rest of Oxford life, can err by trying to cram too much into pupils so that there is little space to absorb the riches on offer.

Some students from an evangelical background find academic theology, with its critical probing of the Bible and its insistence that the development of Christian doctrine cannot be insulated from non-Christian influences, a disturbing experience. Here the liberality of my home religion, which took questioning in its stride, stood me in good stead. Moreover I was able to see that the exercise of critical reasoning was not incompatible with faith, from the example of those who lectured to us. Christopher

Evans, Cuthbert Simpson and Kenneth Woollcombe were not only stimulating lecturers but also known as outstanding preachers, pastors and confessors. If in them heart and mind could be so effectively united, there was really nothing to fear for our faith.

Although the Honours School of Theology was, in those days, somewhat narrowed down to a careful study of biblical texts followed by the most cautious excursion into the very earliest history of Christian doctrine, I found my faith deepened and enlarged. Never again would I treat the Bible as some oracle detached from the life of the community whose members wrote it, preserved it and expounded it. Once you look carefully at the Bible you discover, not only that it is a library of books with all the variety of a good library, but that these books show evidence of being worked over again and again by many hands. These samples of the life of a people were not frozen into immobility but put to use, and applied again and again to ever new situations. Certainly there was something which united this disparate material, a belief that in and amongst the life of this people, with its stories of glory and shame, the mystery of God was to be encountered. In this I was given a clue to the fundamental nature of this curious Christian enterprise. It was not essentially a book, or a doctrine, or an elaborate organization but a stream of life. In it because it truly passed through all too human time and space, there was lots of rubbish, the old boots and cans of human sin about which the Bible stories were remarkably frank, but in it also there was carried the treasure of the good news about God. So, if you wanted that treasure, you could not stay on the bank fastidiously fishing out the edifying bits you liked, you had to risk diving into the stream and allowing yourself to be carried by it. If you were wise you would, of course, try to steer clear of the rubbish.

Once you take seriously this movement of the people of

God through history, you have to face up to the fact of development. If a twentieth-century Christian were to take a time machine and arrive back in an assembly of the early Church, or if one of the first believers were to arrive in one of our parish churches, we should both be amazed. Far more than language or dress would be different; we would encounter a real gulf between our respective ways of thinking and behaving. Indeed there are some Christians who have tried to step back into the past to re-produce the style of worship, doctrine and organization of this primitive Church but it has proved a sadly artificial exercise. More creative have been those who, carried in the stream of life, have genuinely inhabited their own age. If you pay attention to the sheer variety of New Testament literature and, instead of lumping it all together in a sort of theological summer pudding, you savour the different ways in which each writer struggled to respond to the impact of Jesus of Nazareth, then you will begin to grasp something of the excitement of Christian development. This enterprise did not pour off the production line fully equipped for ever and ever; if the basic data were given in the explosive living, dying and rising of Jesus, what happened was so overwhelming that these believers were, like us confronted by some great experience, at a loss for words. Language, images and ideas all fell short of what had been given, and had now to be battered and bent into new shapes to bear adequate witness to what God had done. Time for reflection was needed to get it right. As I studied the history of this pondering, I increasingly admired those bold thinkers who, while affirming their Jewish roots, took the risky course of breaking out of purely traditional ways of thinking and exploited the cultural resources of the Graeco-Roman world. This was not a complicating of a once simple Gospel but the search to do justice to the unsearchable riches of Christ.

Oxford converted me to the task of doing theology, not

just as a three-year exercise to be followed by a return to some allegedly "simple faith", but as a life-time's work. From home I had learned that, in the end, only practical Christianity mattered, that all our talk had to be cashed in terms of love. From my later experience of sacramental worship my imagination was captured through sign and symbol, which satisfied my deepest human needs. But now I had to ask whether what was beautiful was also true. As we knew from the nightmare of Nazism, the imagination could be captured by hideous illusion. Christianity has always been a faith committed to fighting the battle of truth against error, and I knew that I must be involved in that battle so that it was possible for heart and mind to walk in harmony. I knew that there were Christians who managed to hold a naive fundamentalist faith along with a sophisticated acceptance of the discoveries of modern science, but I could already see that this was a potentially disintegrating position which threatened to tear a person into pieces. In more recent years we have seen how, in reaction to over-cerebral cut-down versions of Christianity, there has been a retreat from reasonable faith into various forms of fundamentalism. This trend, along with the activities of bizarre non-Christian cults, reveals modern man, not as the hard-headed, white-coated scientist he imagines himself to be, but as being as superstitious and gullible as any of his ancestors. If it is the imagination which is first captured by faith and the heart which first responds, a complete and secure faith requires the mind to discriminate and to sift. Since Oxford days I have never felt tempted to denigrate rational theology, however much some of its practitioners have seemed to assault the faith of the simple. In truth the simple are nothing like as simple as either superior liberals or nervous orthodox seem to imagine and, in any case, the answer to bad theology is not no theology but better theology.

On the advice of many friends I went for the final stage of my preparation for ordination to Cuddesdon Theological College. Kenneth Clark, who had greatly appreciated its Tractarian sanity and strong spiritual framework, particularly influenced my decision. Edward Knapp-Fisher, then the Principal, was determined to draw a firm line between seminary existence and undergraduate life in Oxford just down the hill. Withdrawal, he believed, was necessary for our formation as men of God. I am bound to say that we often found this somewhat burdensome, not just because we hankered after the fleshpots of the university, but also because National Service had alerted us to the deep gulf which existed between the Church and English society. We were uncomfortable at being detached upon a hill, however holy, from what we called "real life". I remember pacing the college croquet lawn and catching the distinct smell of paint which wafted up to us from the Cowley Motor works and feeling this gulf acutely. Students in those days were much influenced by the writings of those French catholics who had discovered France as a mission field, and were responding to this situation by the renewal of parish life and the development of the worker-priest movement. Yet since then I have come to see that Edward Knapp-Fisher's priorities were the right ones for, however dry the bones of daily office, meditation and Eucharist might seem to be, and however disastrous a purely fundamentalist reproduction of the Cuddesdon system in parish life might prove, I was to find that it was these disciplines which saw me through many a dry and difficult time. Bones need the addition of flesh and the breath of life yet, without them, the body would simply collapse in a soggy mess. What I have seen of theological colleges which, in the unremitting pursuit of relevance, have removed such props, has not been encouraging. The seminary experience is necessarily limited and it is foolish to try to pack too much into it; better far to concentrate on the essential task of trying to overcome the division between the heaven-bent heart and the critical mind by marrying prayer to theology. This is the only way for the Gospel to cease to be a string of words and formulae and to become assimilated and real for the ordinand. In the single-minded pursuit of this task a preachable faith is forged. Of course there will be many gaps to be filled, but there is a life-time of learning still ahead and if eyes and ears are open, parishioners will teach us more than enough "real life".

So Cuddesdon provided me with the opportunity to get my thinking fitted into the sort of framework which my ill-organized attempts at prayer so badly needed. There were enormous gaps in my reading and I found that, with the aid of a well-stocked library, I was able to edge forward beyond the Council of Chalcedon and even savour the writings of modern theologians like Paul Tillich and Rudolph Bultmann. My greatest discovery was the nineteenth-century Anglican, Frederick Dennison Maurice. Compared with the crystal clarity of Newman's writings, his are convoluted and, at times, maddeningly obscure, and yet I found his two-volume *The Kingdom of Christ* well worth the labour. Maurice had been brought up a Unitarian but, in becoming an Anglican, he saw in the doctrine of God as Holy Trinity an expression of the divine unity far richer than what he called "the mathematical worship of the bare number one"; a unity which was able to embrace the real diversity of the "persons" of Father, Son and Holy Spirit. This trinitarian vision was to become the inspiration of Maurice's ecumenism and care for social justice. Loathing all sects and parties for sealing into separate containers the riches of Christendom, he yet perceived what divided Churches were trying to affirm and believed that they naturally belonged together within the catholic framework of the "ordinances of the Kingdom". In our affirmations there was no cause for division; only our negations divided.

With the same passionate belief that diversity and fellowship were not incompatible, Maurice laboured for justice and social unity. The Manchester School of economics set forth competition, the law of the market, as the iron rule of the universe, the way things really are. Maurice denied this, for, he claimed that if you take God seriously, not just as a beautiful idea, but as he who is most really real, then you will know that the ultimate reality is that of the divine diversity in unity. Co-operation not competition is the rule of the universe. This led Maurice to take some very practical steps. After he had made contact with the feared leaders of the 1845 Chartist demonstration, he identified himself with the infant Co-operative Movement and became a pioneer in the field of adult education. I saw in Maurice a theologian whose bold inclusive catholicism blended together the search for Christian and human unity. What was being worked out on the ground at St Matthew Moorfields was here given a theological grounding.

THREE

Ordination and Marriage

When, in 1959, the time came for my ordination to the diaconate, I was offered a job by Ron Treasure, the Vicar of St Michael and All Angels, North Hull. I responded warmly to Ron's pastorally centred understanding of priesthood, his concern for individuals and his conviction that institutions mattered only if they served people. His parish covered a bleak pre-war slum clearance estate, in which row upon row of houses were gathered into avenues which no one had even got round to naming. We had to be content with numbers – Number One Avenue and so on. This bleakness not only revealed desperate human problems but concealed lives of great charity, cheerfulness and even holiness. But this is to anticipate; before I could take up Ron's offer, I had to be accepted by the bishop, Michael Ramsey, newly translated from Durham. As an ordinand from the West Country, I was invited to stay the night at the his riverside home for my interview. Sitting with Joan Ramsey while the Archbishop was working, I must have shown apprehension at the strange rumbling sounds which came from the study above. "That", she said, "is Michael reading. He often runs round the room."

Michael Ramsey is not the easiest of conversationalists which, for the shy ordinand, could be quite an obstacle, but once you can touch on a subject which fires his interest, he comes alive and the wit and wisdom pour forth. Mercifully in my deacon's essay I had referred to the writings of F.D. Maurice, and it was a great relief to find that the Archbishop shared my enthusiasm. Michael Ramsey's

heology has been of great importance to me. He stands
within what is sometimes called the "Liberal Catholic"
stream of Anglican thought, in which the Tractarian
waters meet the more central stream of Maurice,
Westcott, Hort and Lightfoot. In this tradition critical
biblical scholarship is married to the sacramentalism and
spirituality of the Oxford Movement, and in it I felt and
still feel most at home. Sadly it has seemed in danger of
drying up in the Church of England, but I was later to
recognize its essential features in much post-Vatican 2
Roman Catholic theology. But at that time it was
wonderful to have as one's bishop a thinker so profound.
In his Confirmation addresses in our housing estate
church, the Archbishop showed how truly deep thought
could make you profoundly simple. Although no expert
with small talk at the social gatherings which followed
these occasions, he won the hearts of the people by sitting
and looking cheerfully patriarchal and communicating the
fact that he was pleased to be amongst them and cared for
them.

The Archbishop was equally loved and trusted by his
clergy, for he neither thrust upon hard-pressed pastors the
burden of episcopal bright ideas and blueprints nor overtly tried to improve them. We all needed improvement
but, like all human beings resisted being improved too
obviously. As an academic, Michael Ramsey did not pretend to know how to run a parish better than experienced
parish priests, but he did boldly set before us great ideals
of priesthood, his concern always that we should be drawn
more deeply into the one priesthood of Jesus, our great
High Priest.

So, with his wise words ringing in our ears and his hands
laid upon us, ordination, to the diaconate in 1959, and to
the priesthood in 1960, were great occasions. As will be
seen later, not betraying the reality of what happened and
yet coming to terms with Rome's rejection of Anglican

orders, has been one of the most difficult things I have had to do. Everything in York Minster proclaimed continuity with the Church of the past, underlining the intention of the Church of England to "continue, reverently use and esteem" the orders of ministers in Christ's Church. A just assessment of the English Reformation needs to take seriously both the elements of continuity and discontinuity in it. If it is true that some Anglicans have tended to overlook the clear discontinuities involved in the distancing of the order of Holy Communion from the old Mass expressed, sometimes violently, in the breaking of altars and the destruction of eucharistic vestments, it is also true that the Roman judgement on Anglican orders does less than justice to the explicitly stated intention of continuity. Indeed, if we recognize Christ as the living Lord of his Church then we have to introduce a factor more decisive than the sad tale of human faithlessness. Ought we not to question whether, not because of our merits but because of the divine mercy, it is quite as easy to slip wholly out of catholic unity as we had imagined? The achievement of such remarkable agreement on the ministry by the Anglican-Roman Catholic International Commission (ARCIC) could be read as evidence of this divine refusal to let go.

Fully convinced of the reality of my commissioning by God, I embarked upon my ministry to discover the demands and excitements of parish work. Despite the fact that few of our parishioners ever darkened the doors of their church, the pastoral demands were considerable, for many still looked to us for comfort and support in times of need. Clearly the fact that the Church of England has so many non-playing members constitutes an unsatisfactory state of affairs but it does provide its ministers with opportunities to make the love of God a bit more real. This way in which the Church of England has blended together mission and pastoral care produces a form of evangelism which treats people as individuals and not simply victims of a high pressure advertising campaign. Although I was to become a critic of the established status of the national church, I have never wavered in my conviction that this church of the open doors bears more clearly the marks of Christ than any tightly organized in-group which advertises "members only". The Church of the Pure, designed exclusively for spiritual athletes, has never had much attraction for me; indeed, when critics of its mediocrity grind on about the institutional church, I find myself thankful that it has often been its dull officers, the bishops, who have saved the church from the sectarianism of the more exciting prophets and charismatics. If the Gospel is like oil gushing up from the earth, it has required unattractive but solid pipes to get it where it is most needed – to the spiritually poor and empty.

My work for the next three years was the bread and butter of parochial life, visiting people in their homes, especially the sick and elderly, baptizing, marrying, burying and, as was the lot of curates in those days, struggling to hold together a wild open youth club, which lived off the coffee bar and the record player hammering out the then popular "rock 'n' roll". At times, everything got rather out of hand, especially when the lads came off the trawlers the worse for drink. In such crises effective action was taken, not by the curate, but by the stout motherly lady who presided over the coffee bar.

Perhaps most clearly etched on my memory were the long hours, in the early months of the year, spent driving in undertakers' large black cars, to and from the cemetery or crematorium. I especially warmed to the widow who declined burial for her husband in the former, on the grounds that it was too damp for one who had suffered from rheumatics. I have always found difficulty in speaking convincing words of comfort in times of bereavement. Faced with some particularly tragic loss, like the death of a child, my words seem to ring more hollow than usual. In this I was much helped by the way in which north country neighbours instinctively respond to a death. Instead of the cold, cruel, middle class habit of leaving the bereaved to the privacy of their grief, they frankly make of it a social occasion; as tongue-tied as I was, they saw it as their neighbourly duty to call, to be there, and, brewing endless cups of tea, to allow the bereaved to go through again and again the harrowing details of "his last moments". What is good therapy is equally good theology, for it articulates the essence of the incarnation. God does not just send in messages of love; he is there amongst us, sharing our griefs and carrying our sorrows. The defence of this precious truth was to become central to my journey of faith. But back in Hull the lesson was underlined by the advice of my confessor, Father Douglas Carter, then parish priest of St Alban's. "Do not worry too much about what you say. As long as you visit with prayer, your being there is the best witness to the incarnate God." I was beginning to learn something of the sacramental nature of my priesthood, that it was not just a matter of celebrating sacraments but of myself being a sacrament of Christ's presence amongst his people in their need.

Because of the difficulty of finding accommodation for curates on a council housing estate, I had to make do with digs. The limitations of a small bed-sitter were amply compensated for by my landlady, Nana Clarke. She was a remarkable person; widowed early in life she had, single-handed, struggled to bring up her family. As well as running the home she had done every imaginable rough job, from being a lavatory attendant to labouring as a docker during the First World War. On my return from church in the mornings she would feed me with enormous breakfasts of fried bacon and black pudding, all the while keeping going a flow of racy gossip about the neighbourhood. Yet hers was never malicious gossip, it simply

44

reflected an intense interest in and care for the people of the locality. Down the street lived a lonely coloured man, whose legs were covered with terrible sores; it was Nana who every day, despite the fact that her feet were killing her, plodded down the street to wash and dress those ulcers. Although it would be nice to complete the story by saying that Nana was a pillar of the local church, in fact she was not, yet she and many other nonchurchgoers like her taught me an important lesson about the presence and activity of God. Certainly the gifts of the Spirit were distributed amongst members of our congregation, but it seemed that God had gone on to scatter them rather more widely. While the parish priest encounters much evidence of sin, he also keeps meeting goodness breaking out in all sorts of unexpected places and so is given perpetual reminders that God retains his freedom and goes where he will. If the world is stained by evil, it also continues to be bombarded with grace. Later I was to encounter, in the writings of the Jesuit Karl Rahner, a rich vision of the world as the theatre of God's grace, and a sensitive perception of the unconscious response to that grace by those he called "anonymous Christians". It is a matter of debate whether Rahner chose a wise description but, however described, it is there for all with eyes to see and requires an understanding of the Church, not as the sole fortress of goodness, but as the city whose gates are open to the world.

Sadly there was not much ecumenical activity in North Hull. I suspect that in the 1950s the Church of England, inspired by the ideals of the liturgical movement, was concentrating on building up the people of God around the Eucharist. Valuable though this was, it did make us a bit turned in on ourselves. I found more scope for my political interests and joined a New Left group which used to meet in the upstairs room of a local pub. Sipping our half-pints of bitter, we would listen to empassioned doctrinal arguments between Marxists and Trotskyites. Bemused by the subtle nuances of the debate, I could see what Christian doctrinal disputes looked like to outsiders. But these were exciting days for the Labour movement. At Scarborough, Frank Cousins had won his victory for unilateralism, and Hugh Gaitskell had countered with his famous "fight and fight and fight again" speech. I remember taking Ron's wife Liza to hear Hugh Gaitskell speak one Sunday afternoon. Several of my C.N.D. friends were outside the hall giving the Labour leader a rough reception, and I found my pacifist views challenged by the recognition that there lay a deep gulf between moral protest and the discovery of ways and means to achieve one's goal. While remaining a firm supporter of C.N.D. for pointing the clear direction in which we should move, I came to believe that Hugh Gaitskell was more convincing when it came to spelling out the next practical steps in this direction. Much later my irritation with the Labour Party's lust for theoretical debate in the political wilderness, and its failure to hold on to its traditional undoctrinaire supporters, was to lead me to become one of those "defectors" who believed that the time had come to work for a new alignment of the left.

In 1962 there came an invitation from the new Principal of Cuddesdon, Robert Runcie, to return to the college as a member of the staff. The appointment was initially as Chaplain to the college and assistant curate at the parish church, a combination which, the Principal assured me, would be of "sociological" as well as theological significance. Robert Runcie certainly knew how to produce the sort of job description which might entice a curate, who felt mildly guilty about abandoning work in a northern city for what looked liked the gentler pastures of an Oxfordshire village. Allowing myself to be caught by the Runcie bait I never regretted it. In fact the idyllic image of Cuddesdon is highly misleading; most men worked, not

n farms, but in the nearby Cowley Motor works, and the
ocial character of the village was shown, at that time, by
he extraordinary percentage of its population which held
aid up membership of the Labour Party. In fact the Party
Christmas Bazaar was a more genuine expression of vil-
age life than the summer Fête, which was overdependent
n the efforts of students. Although our parishioners felt
hat the churchyard was the place to which "we all come
ome", church attendance was as meagre as it had been in
Iull. Indeed there was a whiff of anti-clericalism in the
ir, stirred, no doubt, by the slightly oppressive presence
f so many clergymen or aspiring clergymen but, despite
his, demands on them were unabated. A succession of
aintly curates had set a breath-taking pace of pastoral
ctivity. I am afraid that I was never able to rise to the
eights of my predecessor, who was the regular "caller" at
he weekly Bingo sessions and who could be seen at
ehearsals for the village pantomime correcting Greek
xercises in the wings as he waited to go on stage as
Buttons. The heaviest demands fell on Robert Runcie,
vho had the impossible job of being both principal of a
heological college and vicar. He was quite without
astidiousness about parochial chores, whether it was visit-
ng, teaching at the local school or going on the Sunday
chool outing to the seaside, and there are many folk in
he village who can testify to his devoted, time-consuming
are as a pastor in times of need. Sunday by Sunday we
vould take the sacrament to the sick straight from the
arish Eucharist. One old lady, although she walked the
illage street with an alarm clock suspended around her
eck, had become so confused about time that we would
rrive with the blessed sacrament to find her, carving
nife in hand, poised over the Sunday joint.

Significant developments took place during this period
n the life of the college. Robert Runcie is, by nature, a
raditional person who loves and respects the past yet,

while seeing himself as the servant of all that the colleg
had stood for, he knew that there had to be movement. I
was the time of the 1960s theological explosion dominate
by Bishop John Robinson's *Honest to God* and the mor
sober volume of Cambridge essays *Soundings*. The bubbl
of a somewhat complacent biblical theology and liturgica
movement was burst, and we were made to recogniz
that, beneath the mild post-war religious boom, there la
unresolved theological problems and stark pastora
realities. It was not good enough to string together a
assortment of biblical texts and slap them on the counter
when the consumer was really asking what we meant b
the word "God", which we trotted out so casually. It wa
not good enough to go on pretending that the nation wa
Christian at heart, simply waiting to be gathered togethe
as the Family of God for the Lord's own service on th
Lord's own day. We needed to start far further back, t
take far less for granted. Indeed, if like the Bishop o
Woolwich we were honest, we would recognize that th
problem of belief was not just a problem for "them" bu
could be traced back into ourselves; we too were th
wistful half-believers. Of course, to those who had read
bit of modern theology, what the Bishop had to say wa
nothing very new. What was startling was that here wa
something more than the seminar speculations of a
academic, a pastoral missionary bishop, laid up wit
a slipped disc, bringing to the surface a number of th
uncertainties we hardly dared to voice. The shock wa
salutary because, even if the Bishop did not get th
answers right, he forced us to face the fundamenta
question, the reality of God. When, undisturbed, we tal
too easily about God, we are in danger of treating him a
an object like the old ornament on the mantelpiece, whic
is always there but rarely noticed. Indeed in gli
orthodoxy there is much hidden unbelief. The *Honest t
God* debate made us sit up and take notice but, havin

done this, we could move in a number of different
directions. We could bang the door on further questioning
and retire back to the safety of the old slogans. We could
fashion a brand new religion in which all talk about God
was reduced to thinly disguised talk about man, so that, to
say "God is love" is really to announce that love is the
ultimate standard we have chosen. Or we could do the
exciting and creative thing, rediscover the overwhelming
mystery of God. If all our talk about God was necessarily
expressed in human and so inadequate words, yet they
could truly point to that mystery which has been declared
to us in the person of Jesus. We would have to talk about
God more carefully, not because there was nothing really
to talk about, but because he is simply too much for the
earthen vessels of our words.

The impact of *Honest to God*, with the notorious
newspaper headline "Your image of God must go", was
considerable, and for many students the foundations were
truly rocked. It was with extraordinary sensitivity and
sure-footedness that Robert Runcie dealt with the
situation. The issues had to be faced and students equipped with the skills to do this. So Robert set out to
provide the college with a somewhat sharper intellectual
edge. Men of the calibre of Mark Santer were brought
onto the staff and we began to make greater use of the
theological resources of Oxford. David Jenkins, then at
the Queen's College, led a remarkable series of doctrine
seminars in which students were helped to discriminate
between the serious issues and superficial froth, while Dr
Dillistone, from Oriel, opened eyes to the religious quest
in contemporary secular literature. After a highly original
course of Holy Week lectures in the parish church, an
elderly episcopal resident of the village was to be seen
hunting for the plays of Arthur Miller in the devotional
section of Mowbrays bookshop. While encouraging men
to face the intellectual challenge, Robert Runcie knew

that, if all the furniture were moved around at once, if there were no stable framework, the fearful would lose their nerve and bolt for safety, so he insisted on a certain institutional conservatism to provide the security necessary for the probing of new problems.

It was my task to teach the bread and butter of Christian doctrine. I was woefully inadequate but discovered the old truth that there is nothing like teaching to make you learn. What I tried to do was to get students to see that all this formidable torrent of Christian words was about things which really mattered to the people they would meet in their parishes. While welcoming the fresh air blown into our studies by the *Honest to God* debate, I was becoming aware of some of the dangers. A radical theologian who came to lecture at the college saw God as a source of alienation, coming between man and man, and declared that the altars standing in our churches were symbols of this. That night a student dreamt that we came into the college chapel to be confronted, not by the altar, but a large mirror. Our worship consisted of simply gazing at ourselves. That put the danger very precisely. If God-talk were just disguised talk about ourselves, we were left shut up in the human dilemma. While it was all very well, on the croquet lawn of an Oxfordshire village, to luxuriate in the thought that love and beauty are the ultimate realities, what of poor suffering humanity whose situation hardly encouraged such a belief? Did not their experience tell them that indifference and lovelessness had the last word? The Gospel surely came as a surprise to lumpen shepherds on a hillside, the last thing they had expected God come near in a helpless child. If we had anything to offer to the unspiritual and bogged down, it could not be insights bubbling up in the minds of a spiritual élite, but that which came from outside our situation, the self-disclosing of God in Jesus. Whether we had good news or not depended on the doctrines of revelation and incarnation. Of course it was possible to mount powerful arguments against these doctrines, but then they were arguments against Christianity itself. Neither belief or unbelief were taken seriously by those who swallowed the critique and then indulged in a sentimental salvage operation of a few cultural remnants of the faith. This simply led to the grossest conservatism of continuing to drink the institutional bathwater while letting go of the Babe.

While providing sufficient structure for the college, Robert Runcie relaxed some of its rigidities and broke its strained celibate mould. After all, some students were married and most would become so: keeping women at a distance was both unrealistic and stressful. Wives, fiancées and girl friends became acceptable, and members of the staff were amongst the early beneficiaries of this relaxation. Hard on the heels of the Vice-Principal, Mark Santer and I were to follow into marriage. Hilary Lord was an old friend of Lindy Runcie and, working as a librarian at the Bodleian in Oxford, she was a frequent visitor to Cuddesdon. When Lindy went into hospital to have her second baby, it was arranged that Hilary should come to look after young James Runcie. His father asked me to keep an eye on this lone girl set down in such a monastic world, and I carried out my duties diligently and enthusiastically. I am a slow mover in most things, but although we had only met in the summer, I had proposed and been accepted in the autumn, and we were married in the following February. So my life was given a whole new dimension and I experienced a completeness which I had not known before.

While accepting the creativity of celibacy for the sake of the Gospel, and indeed the need for the mobility and availability of those who follow this vocation, I could not help noticing that there are some for whom an enforced celibacy leads to a diminishment of humanity. In truth the

Church should be starry-eyed neither about marriage nor about celibacy, for both vocations have their own problems and opportunities. Grace does amazing things but, we are told, grace perfects nature; God has to work on us as we really are. I am by nature a lonely person, reticent about opening up with confidence even to my closest friends, so that, thrown in upon myself I can become introspective and brooding. I have no doubt that I have needed Hilary to make me a bit more complete. Mercifully she has never felt a special vocation to be a vicar's wife; any invitation to arrange flowers in church or run some women's organization, has filled her with foreboding. But her rejection of an official role has set her free to be wholly with me at the level where it matters, and to provide a home which is both a refuge and yet open to all manner of visitors. When our children, James and Elizabeth, were born, Hilary had the nerve and determination to see home creation for what it is, an important and absorbing task. For this, the three of us have reason to be deeply grateful.

While the waters of the Church of England were being stirred by the *Honest to God* debate, the Second Vatican Council of the Roman Communion was beginning to lay before us the fruits of its deliberations. Anglicans were moved by the warmth and openness of Pope John, and were encouraged by the two great decrees of November 1963, on the Church and on Ecumenism. Here was a change of emphasis. The Council was struggling for words to express what Pope John had expressed in gesture. It was reaching out to throw its arms around not only the "separated brethren", but those of other great religions, and indeed around the whole world. The fortress Church was being dismantled. I remember how in Oxford we caught a breath of this wind of change when Hans Küng, the lively theologian of Tübingen, came to lecture. If Rome were to become the Rome of Küng that would be something, for it would mean its conversion to Anglican values. Frankly, at that time, many of us judged the Council by the extent to which it seemed to move in our direction. No wonder we were disappointed when we stubbed our toes yet again on the rock of Roman intransigence. The Catholic Church "subsisted" in those churches in communion with Rome. Vatican 1, with its troublesome proclamation of papal infallibility, although now set in a wider context, the Pope amidst the College of Bishops, was not withdrawn. Clearly there were still problems.

FOUR

Silksworth and Chadwick

Much as I appreciated my spell of teaching at Cuddesdon, I was becoming restless to get back to full parochial life. I loved doing theology, but felt that my study needed to be fed as much by pastoral work as by books. There was already talk about the gulf which was alleged to lie between the theologian and parish priest, and I saw this as a personal challenge to return to parish work, and there to go on trying to be a theologian.

At this time I was to meet a Cuddesdon priest, Gordon Hopkins, the Rural Dean of Sunderland, and vicar, for many years, of the ship-building parish of Pallion. Here was a proper parish priest, one of the glories of the Church of England, who, although immersed in the life of his neighbourhood, continued to read and think. It was through Gordon that I was drawn to become Vicar of Silksworth, a parish on the outskirts of Sunderland.

There were elaborate plans for this colliery village to become part of a new township with an additional population of some twenty thousand. When it was discovered that the population projection for Sunderland was in error, the scheme was somewhat modified and instead of becoming a new town pioneer, I was to be the vicar of a very traditional County Durham colliery. As the population of the so-called village was already about twelve thousand, there was plenty to do, and I can now see that Silksworth as it was provided me with a task more congenial and manageable than the new township would have done.

Nobody can pretend that Silksworth is easy on the eye;

containing its fair share of sub-standard houses, and with a sharp wind from the North Sea stirring up the litter of old fish and chip papers, it could look fairly desolate. Yet it was a humane and good community. A housing policy, wiser than that which had surrounded Sunderland with new estates, concentrated on the demolition and rebuilding of whole streets, which meant that the fabric of the community, with its extended families and neighbourliness, was not destroyed. Allowing old working class communities to be broken up through insensitive housing policies or the idolatry of those market forces which require the endless chasing of jobs, has been a folly beyond belief. It is simply no good crying for those common values which hold a nation together when you destroy the very communities which are the preservers and communicators of such values. The culture, the way of life, of a colliery may not be perfect; you certainly cannot ignore the hard drinking, the conformism and the conservative adhesion to old ways, which while congenial to the elderly, frustrates the young and enterprising. But, warts and all, here is a way of life, carefully built up over the years, which holds people together, teaches them to depend on one another and is intolerant of crime and violence directed against that community. This precious fabric could be destroyed almost overnight. During the 1984 miners' strike, nothing was so frustrating as the inability of the governing classes of the South-East, to perceive this dimension of the problem. It was pure hypocrisy to permit the destruction of this chosen way of life while the taxpayers' money was being shelled out to preserve that of the Falkland islanders.

Hilary and I, inescapably southerners, were privileged to have the opportunity to learn from a way of life different from our own. The standard of living in the North-East is visibly lower than that of the South. Even in the early seventies, when we left Silksworth, male unemployment in the area stood at twelve per cent. This meant that expectations were not unduly high, and people suspected that whatever prosperity might be achieved was always at risk. Such realism gives to the communities of the North-East an admirable resilience. After all, life is not all work; there are allotments to be tended, whippets to be exercised, pigeons to be raced, working men's clubs to be joined, and the challenge of producing for the Leek Show the grossest vegetable of all. Faced with this rich and good humoured way of life, Hilary and I realized the absurdity and diminishment of class divisions. Here were lessons which the nation could not afford to deny itself by persisting in such cultural apartheid.

In Silksworth we were given the opportunity to discover something of the glories and frailties of the Labour movement. At the Miners' Gala it might be my privilege to lead the colliery band into Durham Cathedral for the gala service, after marching behind the banner with the Lodge officials and attending the political speeches on the race course. There was something of a gap between the heady rhetoric of the speakers and the less than sober reality that most participants preferred to enjoy the opportunities of extended licensing hours. The overwhelming dominance of the Labour Party in the county bred a rather complacent establishmentarianism and even petty tyranny. Yet I developed a profound respect for many pillars of the party. Their vision of society, not as a ladder up which individuals climb to get away from the less successful, but as a community of mutual responsibility, was a noble one. It was the political expression of that practical neighbourliness which we met every day in our streets. With its roots deeper in the Christian tradition of the chapels than in Marxist theory, it was light years away from those middle class discussions in a Hull pub, where we argued whether Trotsky was a heretic or not. It is the damage done to the advocates of this tradition which is the saddest feature of the advance in recent years of the hard militant left.

Although our congregation at St Matthew's was small, church and vicar occupied a real niche in the community. As the church was at one end of the village and my vicarage at the other, I had to walk up and down the main street several times each day, which gave me a wonderful opportunity to chat with all and sundry. Since returning to the South, it has been a shock to discover that here one is not expected to pass the time of day with strangers. There were occasions when the community would rally to the parish church. The death of a miner could mean a procession down the village street, led by the colliery band and the Lodge banner. When Lord Attlee died, we had a memorial service at which Bishop Ian Ramsey preached, and the N.U.M. officials and local M.P. attended. It was important to keep the church open to all these barely articulate rediscoveries of Christian roots but, at the same time, to have a firm heart as well as open arms. So at the heart of our life was a congregation centred on the Eucharist, small but passionately loyal. While the media see Bishops and Synods as the face of the Church, God, I venture to think, sees the faces of folk like Mary, the verger, whose passion for cleanliness could send her out amidst the wedding congregation poised to greet the bride, to remove some offending cobweb; like Bob, a gentle, white-haired giant who had taught himself to paint and play the flute; George, the churchwarden, with whom a succession of clergy would drink and laugh, and on whose wisdom we so much depended. He, with Jean his wife, were regular weekday communicants. These were the real Church and they, with splendid curates like Stuart Nattrass and Tim Ollier, provided us with support and friendship.

Silksworth contained a variety of churches, each of which had, in the past, a distinct sociological base. Thus the parish church had served the few neighbouring gentry and farmers, the Wesleyans, and colliery officials and shopkeepers, the Primitive Methodists the trades unionists, and the Roman Catholics the small community of immigrant Irish labourers. Of course these sharp edges had become somewhat blurred, but it was only just prior to our arrival that the Primitive Methodist chapel had been closed, leaving a small body of dissidents, who could not countenance the Wesleyan tradition, to transfer their allegiance to the fiercely revivalist Independent Methodist chapel.

Our arrival in Silksworth coincided with the "People Next Door" Campaign, which in the colliery proved to be a highly successful first step in local ecumenism. Thanks to the efforts of the local clergy it had the lasting result of producing a number of house groups made up of Methodists, Roman Catholics and Anglicans, which were to prove the solid basis of our future work together. It was wonderful to be able to work in close harmony with both the Methodist minister, Ken Mankin, and the Catholic priest, James Burke. This full Catholic participation in our efforts showed us all how effective the Second Vatican Council could be at the local level. Father Burke, trained in the old ways but welcoming the new openness without in any way losing his roots in the past, proved a supportive colleague and personal friend. He introduced Hilary and me to the splendour of the Durham countryside and, as he drove us through the county, would make frequent diversions so that we could enjoy the hospitality of his many friends and relations. Sometimes clergy complain that they can get nowhere with the ministers of other churches. Of course, if we approach one another bearing invitations to yet more ecclesiastical activity, the weary and hard pressed may respond with less than enthusiasm, but if we start by forging the bonds of personal friendship then all manner of doors will open.

In Silksworth these doors were opening and we were all enjoying the experience, all, that is, except the Independent Methodists, who remained stubbornly aloof. I did once go and speak at their women's "Bright Hour". After a good deal of hymn singing, I gave my address on our Lord's longing for the unity of his followers. The lady president arose and said: "We thank our brother for his words. There were so many things in it with which I disagreed that I cannot mention them all now, but will do so afterwards over tea." Whereupon there appeared teapots, sandwiches and cream cakes, and I discovered that the main stumbling block was seen, not as bishops or popes, but my failure to speak out on the evils of drink. None the less, even in this direction, there was some hope in the shape of an annual Temperance Carol Service to which we were all invited. For over two hours we laboured through this marathon event which, by custom, was presided over by the current mayor of Sunderland. One year it was a director of the local brewery while another it was a particularly unecclesiastical dignitary who rounded the evening off with the words: "Now boys and girls, you have all had a good sing and got the phlegm off your bellies!"

It was encouraging that, in this local ecumenism, we were able to produce evidence that we were aiming at something higher than simply huddling together more closely in the face of a hostile world, that our labours for unity were to enable us to serve the world more effectively. We managed to set up a lunch club for social workers, doctors, teachers and others who cared for the locality, whether professionals or volunteers. This proved to be a useful way of improving the channels of communication. When our pit closed, it was proposed that its underground workings should become a dump for toxic industrial waste. While some welcomed the new opportunities this would afford for employment, others were afraid of the potential threat to the community's health. A fierce debate broke out and the churches, instead of taking sides, set up a meeting at which the promoters of the scheme could explain the plans and be exposed to the sharpest questioning. A lively encounter took place in the parish church, with the genial but tough Father Burke holding the ring. Some members of the congregation were shocked at this hurly burly in the house of God but, in the end, most were helped to see that reconciliation is not a matter of evading conflict or simply pouring oil on troubled waters. The Gospel faith calls for an ability to handle the hottest of potatoes. I recognize that this is a lesson which I have constantly to preach to myself for, while there are some who seem to flourish in situations of conflict, I find myself falling over backwards to defuse it. This may be an amiable weakness, but weakness it is none the less, for real peace requires – as the Anglican-Roman Catholic International Commission has shown so admirably – the ability to face disagreement by tracing it back to its source.

I certainly had to face conflict when I became a member of the Archbishops' Commission on Church and State. With any group of people meeting regularly over a period of time, the dice is loaded in favour of consensus, for it becomes a group of friends, but Owen Chadwick, our chairman, had a tough job on his hands with members as diverse as the late Ronald Williams, the Bishop of Leicester, an ardent supporter of establishment, and Valerie Pitt, an equally ardent opponent. He treated us with remarkable forbearance.

I wanted to see the case for disestablishment argued in a way which would avoid any suggestion that the Church of England should become simply a sect of committed believers. As I have maintained in my little book *Church and Nation*, the choice is not between a national established church and a tight in-group which waves its fist at the world, for there are other more creative ways of seeing a church which reconciles the claims of clear Christian identity and openness to the world. I was little interested in making sweeping judgements about the compromises which followed the official recognition of the Church by Constantine, for I recognized that some things, which looked like a dilution of faith, were simply the inevitable price paid for taking the risk of becoming a city with gates open to the world and the variety of its cultures. However, I did believe that the classical argument in favour of the English establishment, Hooker's view of Church and Nation as two sides of one coin, was no longer realistic in a pluralist society with its many brands of belief and unbelief. The disestablishment I sought would be just one stage in the process of coming to terms with the facts of life, one more blow at an illusion which, like all illusions, impedes effective action. Moreover, only by disentangling the ties between church and state could the Church of England become a mature self-governing body, able to choose its own leaders, order its own worship and express its contemporary understanding of faith. The latter issue was to become of increasing importance to me. The ability of the Church of England to express its mind seemed impeded by the fact that the 1662 Prayer Book remained its official statement of faith, and Parliament the final arbiter of what it could do. It seemed to me unsatisfactory that the final court of appeal in some of the great issues which confronted the Church of England, such as the ordination of women or reunion with the Church of Rome, would inevitably be Parliament.

I knew enough about political realities to recognize that there were acceptable as well as unacceptable compromises. It would be good to move a few steps in the right direction and, it must be said, the Commission made proposals which would set church and state rather further apart. The Commission has achieved its objective, for the General Synod now has greater control of worship and there is a deeper church involvement in the appointment of bishops. Although it is safe to assume that Mrs Thatcher has strong views on bishops, she has yet presided over the appointment of several severe thorns in her flesh. However, as we have no means of knowing what more severe thorns the Prime Minister may have rejected, and we know quite clearly, from recent parliamentary debates, that parliament has not abandoned its powers, the traditional Church of England umpires remain firmly in place. They have the decisive say. Moreover the Commission's essential conservatism was betrayed by its unwillingness to question the established status of the national church. By sticking strictly to the laws which affect the Church of England and not other churches, it evaded the question of the status which is acquired as a result of those laws.

At the end of the day I felt compelled to declare my solidarity with Valerie Pitt and Dennis Coe, then Labour M.P. for Middleton, and add a note of dissent. Was this, after my stand as a conscientious objector, just another outburst of my nonconforming spirit? Was I addicted to stepping out of line and indulging in the luxury of irresponsible dissent? I am bound to say that I did not enjoy letting down those with whom I had discussed, laughed and prayed. As we gathered for our final session at Goodwood House, the home of our Vice-Chairman, the Earl of March, I felt wretched at breaking ranks with such good friends.

My membership of the Chadwick Commission is important for this story, as it was during this period that I began to feel a niggle about the Church of Rome. Inevitably I had to look again at the English Reformation and I found increased difficulty in siding with Henry VIII in his rupture of the papal tie which held the Church of England to the universal Church. The individual colour and responsibility of local churches are to be encouraged, but I found myself dissatisfied with any form of merely national Christianity. Indeed the very title Church OF England seemed to blunt the truth that the Church is essentially universal and can only be the church IN this nation or that. As I re-read the story of the Church, I could no longer believe that there existed a sort of primitive English catholicism which was innocent of the papal connection. Popes could be a cause of irritation and resentment but, as far as I could see, the English Church had never, until Henry VIII, thought of dispensing with them. Inconvenient though the papacy might often seem to be, it was assumed to be part of the Christian kit. As Thomas More, a very critical supporter of the papacy, was to say: "The papacy is at least-wise instituted by the corps of Christendom and for a great urgent cause in avoiding of schisms." The nationalization of the Church under Henry VIII I saw as a distortion of its true nature, and I rejoiced in the fact that, through the growth of the Anglican Communion and the experience of ecumenism, the Church of England was moving back towards a more international understanding of Christianity. It was during meetings of the Commission that I first met Bishop Christopher Butler, who was acting as a Roman Catholic observer. I warmed to his evident appreciation of his own Anglican roots and glimpsed in him the real possibilities of being an Anglican Roman Catholic. Since then I have read many of his books and he has seemed to me to be one of the most trustworthy interpreters of Vatican 2, doing justice both to the opening of the Church's doors and to the continuing affirmation of the solid centre of the Christian enterprise in Catholic unity. I know no better book for the intelligent enquirer than his *An Approach to Christianity*.

Membership of the Chadwick Commission proved my baptism into ecclesiastical power politics. Taking evidence from church leaders and, even more awe-inspiringly from the massive Lord Reith, along with an initiation into the mysteries of what went on in 10 Downing Street when bishops were appointed, provided a fascinating and heady experience. In this world, to be effective is to be political and that bluntly means having access to the levers of power. The ghastliness of ecclesiastical politics stems not from the fact that they are political but from the gloss of piety which is applied to prevent them from appearing to be such. But where does the desire to be effective end and personal ambition begin?

The same problem confronted me when I became a member of the General Synod. As my election coincided with the publication of the Commission's report, I found myself supporting the reforms which it had proposed while insisting that the issue of establishment itself was unavoidable. If we really pursued the freedom to order our own worship and doctrine, and if we really wanted to have the decisive voice in the choice of bishops, sooner or later voices would cry that the Church of England could not expect to have its cake and eat it, the privileges of establishment with the liberty of disestablishment. I underestimated the Synod's hidden assumption that the established status quo was the one part of the Church of England's heritage which could not seriously be questioned.

But this was not the only matter to occupy my attention, the Anglican-Methodist Unity Scheme was still on the table and it had my strong support. This had been produced after long and serious theological discussion and, if there was not agreement on every jot and tittle, it showed that the two churches were on converging paths. The scheme, while allowing for a preliminary stage of further growing together, pointed quite unambiguously to the goal of organic unity. We were not content to be just better friends; we wanted to die to separate existence and enter into marriage. This seemed to me to be a genuine attempt to embody catholic inclusiveness. There was a problem about the Service of Reconciliation which would herald the union of the Churches. Did it involve the re-ordination of the non-episcopally ordained Methodist ministers? In the Church of England, Anglo-Catholics believed that it should while Evangelicals believed that it should not, yet, divided as they were, the two parties united in the conviction that the disputed service was unacceptably ambiguous and made common cause against the scheme. To my mind Anglo-Catholics were straining out the gnat and swallowing the camel, risking fuller catholic unity for the sake of a dubious issue. Ambiguity is inevitable in the coming together of separated Christians, for nothing is so odd and ambiguous as their divided state.

Vatican 2, it seemed, had discerned this ambiguity in going beyond the clear cut and comforting insistence that one was either in or out of the Church. While the Catholic Church "subsisted" in those Churches in communion with Rome, it wished to claim that others were still in imperfect communion with this centre. After all, it was not a radical theologian but Pope Paul who had called the Anglican Communion a "sister church". I believed that in considering the problem of uniting divided ministries, we needed to do justice both to the call to become part of a wider unity, whether achieved through the historic episcopate or the papacy, and to the fact that God had undoubtedly used and blessed those ministries divided from that unity. In acknowledging the latter we should not be rather grudgingly recognizing that God occasionally breaks his own rules, but seeing that this is in fact typical of the way he overrules our sin and divisiveness. Anglo-Catholics seemed to be operating with a view of an absentee Lord who had launched his Church, laid down the rules, and then left it to operate in an autonomous way. My evangelical past had taught me a different tale, that of the living Christ who, while ruling his Church through the sacraments of his presence, has not abandoned his freedom to go his own way and to the unexpected. He is the one who continues to deal with us as we are, in our divided state. Thus, if with penitence for our sin and with gratitude for his continued mercy, we came to lay our ambiguous situation at his feet, he could be trusted to put things right. With this conviction, I threw myself into the campaign for Anglican-Methodist unity.

When it failed to achieve a sufficient majority in the Synod, I was forced to look more critically at the realities of Anglican comprehensiveness. On the surface the Church of England looks an ideal vehicle for ecumenism, a bridge between catholic order and the evangelical affirmation of divine grace. Could you not, in the one Church, enjoy both the splendours of pre-Vatican 2 Roman liturgy and the plain sober piety of Geneva? Yet, when faced with a concrete proposal to unite Churches, the whole thing had seemed to blow up in our faces. Was it that the various "parties" in the Church of England had co-existed in a state of lazy comprehensiveness without embarking upon the costly task of reconciliation?

Synodical government in the Church of England, bringing together in conference bishops, priests and laity, is a brave attempt to embody the People of God as something other than a lumpen proletariat receiving orders from a hierarchy above. But it has its weaknesses and dangers. Time does not permit the sort of serious theological reflection which is necessary to trace differences to their roots and achieve genuine agreement. Too often the ringing of the division bell sends members scurrying back into prepared partisan positions, satisfied to accept compromises or those vague formulae which can mean all things to all men. But the greatest danger of synodical government is the way it becomes a burgeoning and all-absorbing industry, so that its enthusiasts really come to believe that the activities of Church House and the Synod are the "centre" of church life. Inevitably all this governing, like the governing of the Vatican, has a higher profile than what goes on in parishes, for what is said and done by these bodies is sometimes newsworthy, but it is fatal if the illusion is believed in. The real life of the Church takes place in the humdrum and anonymous witness of lay people dispersed throughout the world. Unless this sense of priorities is recognized, lay people are sucked from the frontline in the secular world into the shadows of ecclesiastical politics, and their role is subtly devalued.

There was plenty going on in Silksworth to keep my feet on the ground. In 1971 I had the thrill of being present at the birth of our first child, James, in the old Easington workhouse. The medical care Hilary received from our Marxist G.P., Sammy Glatt, and the Baptist gynaecologist, Rex Gardner, could not have been bettered, and the way in which the people of Silksworth shared our happiness was heart-warming.

But for the community there was a sadness ahead, the closure of our pit. Hilary and I had been down it and seen for ourselves the conditions under which men were working. As we crawled on hands and knees to the coal face, which was only a few feet high, we knew that the pit's days were numbered. In those happier days of careful consultation at the local level, the N.C.B. and the N.U.M. co-operated to make the closure as painless as possible; in fact very few miners were made redundant. A rather different picture of labour relations was given that year in the now famous strike. As coal merchants collected their stocks direct from the pits, areas like ours were the first to suffer as fuel shortage was added to power cuts. I recall queuing outside the Co-op for a precious bag of coke to keep the Aga going and the new baby warm.

The most vivid memory of the strike was sitting round the kitchen table preparing a young couple for marriage, enjoying the one source of heat in the house, and our only light a candle. In all this, where we are able to share one another's joys, sorrows and difficulties, lies the true centre of church life. In the perspective of the Kingdom mountains are brought low, the self-important things look small and it is the hidden lives of courage, good humour and love which are the really great things.

FIVE

Barnard Castle

Our days in Silksworth were coming to an end. An offer came from Trinity College, Cambridge of the living of Barnard Castle, a market town on the southern edge of the county. As conscientious patrons, the College had made the offer in close consultation with the Bishop of Durham. Ian Ramsey, who had plans for church life in Teesdale buzzing in his ever fertile mind, was keen that I should make this move and I felt it right to take his advice. As you travel west from Bishop Auckland, you reach a point beyond West Auckland near Raby Castle, where you suddenly encounter a world quite different from the east of the county. Gone is the raw, pit-scarred, east-wind-blown landscape and you enter a gentler, more wooded and prosperous looking countryside, whose prevailing wind is damp and from the west. You feel as if you are in the Yorkshire dales.

"Barny" was the loveliest place in which I have ever lived. The view from our vicarage over the River Tees to the hills of North Yorkshire was a source of constant joy and, as in Silksworth, we were to receive immense kindness from our parishioners. When Elizabeth, our second child, was born prematurely in Darlington Hospital, and for several days hovered between life and death, many good friends rallied to our aid and upheld us. Yet, I am bound to say that I found the work in Barnard Castle hard going. Being the vicar of a market town is thought of as a particularly idyllic existence, but I was to find the taciturn character of dales folk and the subtleties of a socially mixed parish more difficult to cope with than the blunt forthrightness of a working class community.

One of the difficulties of moving from one parish to another is the tendency to go on seeing the new situation through lenses adjusted to the old one. I failed to do what was required, to stand patiently still and listen to the heartbeat of the new parish. Church life had a different tone to it. In the east of the county urban congregations are often small and struggling yet they have a fierce sense that the church is their responsibility and requires their commitment and loyalty. Of course there were church members like this in Barnard Castle, but there was a wider fringe made up of those who saw the church as something to be occasionally turned to rather than actually belonged to. In Teesdale the natural home for what is often called "folk religion" is the Methodist rather than the Anglican church, but because many of the chapels had closed, those with a Nonconformist background often had to turn to the Church of England. Yet their expectations of what was on offer were still shaped by their past. "I'm not a sacramental Christian" was a comment I heard not infrequently. This meant that the Eucharist-centred life which I had taken for granted in Silksworth had still to be struggled for in Barnard Castle.

Other things also could not be taken for granted. While local ecumenism had got off to a spanking pace under a former vicar, Alan Webster (now Dean of St Paul's), it had got into a rut and was beginning to decay. The churches in Barnard Castle tended to erupt into occasional acts of united worship and witness without the backing of any solid and continuing work. It was in this situation that I began to see some of the weaknesses in the policy of intercommunion which I had strongly advocated. The question is asked as to whether the Eucharist is a means to unity or its goal. Taking seriously St Paul's claim that "because there is one loaf, we who are many are one body, for we all partake of the same loaf" (1 Corinthians 10:17), I tended to the former view. If the Eucharist could properly be described as a "means of grace" could it not be a means of this grace of unity? We come to God in all our natural diversity and sinful divisiveness, and he, the architect of unity, acts on us to weld us into one. Was that not what actually happened to those earliest Christians who, with their great variety of ways of understanding Christ and structuring the Church's ministry, came to a common expression of faith in the creeds, and to a common church order through the experience of eucharistic sharing? In Silksworth our experience had been that a point had come in our developing relationship with the Methodists when it had seemed right to yield ourselves to receive deeper unity as a gift from the hands of the living Christ. I believe that in the context of our real commitment to one another and willingness to die to separation, we were on to something important. But in Barnard Castle I was to recognize the danger of what Bishop Lesslie Newbigin once called "promiscuous inter-communion", by which he meant, occasional acts of intercommunion without that underlying commitment and desire for unity. What I was experiencing now was inter-communion practised as an ecumenical demonstration announcing to the world, not "We long to be one", but "Despite all appearances, we really are one".

So I began to understand what was meant by those who rejected the sort of intercommunion which had for years been practised by the Free Churches. It was fundamentally an acquiescence in division, tempting us away from the costly business of dying to separation. What looked like complacency, masked by the rhetoric of ecumenism, troubled me at a time when I was feeling more acutely than ever the horror of schism. You cannot live in dales country without becoming aware of the scars of Christian disunity. As we visited "the bare ruined choirs" of

Fountains, Jervaulx, Easby and Egglestone abbeys, we not only marvelled at their beauty, but, faced with this evidence of a rupture in our Christian past, mourned the tragic negations of the Reformation. Was there not, for all this destruction, some repentance called for? What were the real reasons for continuing to keep these wounds alive? Such deep wounds cried out for healing but they could not be healed lightly by saying "Peace" where there was no peace.

I find that I cannot do pastoral work without being driven further in my theological pilgrimage, for how could one be involved in human problems and one's own struggle to speak about God without intensifying this search of the mind for understanding? Of course the fullness of God's gift had been given in Jesus but, like Mary, we need not only to receive that gift, but to ponder it in our hearts (Luke 2:19). Here I was to discover the point where my poor attempts to understand and to pray met. In my prayer I was being enticed, through words and images, into that silence where God is simply himself and my verbosity was stilled. But, in trying to make this journey into silence, I found that the great questions of faith were raised in a more than theoretical way. Was I fashioning a God shaped to my image and likeness, a mere projection of what I wanted? In moving into prayer could I be sure that I was not just talking to myself? Back from silence I had to return, not simply to more of my own chatter, but to Jesus, the image of the invisible God, the Word made flesh. At this crucial point my faith, and that of those to whom I ministered, depended on there being this break in the clouds, the sun of righteousness glimpsed, God's self-disclosure rescuing us from the man-made gods of our funny little ideas.

This mattered to me more than all the faintly comic fussing and fretting of ecclesiastical organizations, for upon it my very existence as a Christian and a minister of the Gospel depended. I had learned valuable lessons from the *Honest to God* debate, but was becoming increasingly dissatisfied with the game of cowboys and indians which journalists were setting up between liberals and conservatives. I could see Christian words and images reduced to mere human guesses about God, leaving such a banal and superficial remnant of faith that it was no wonder some priests sought to be useful by pretending to be social workers or psychiatrists. I could see too the sad but inevitable reaction to this, a burying of the Gospel in nostalgic old-fashionedness. It was F.D. Maurice who had warned of the danger of opposing "the spirit of the age" with "the spirit of a former age". There were so-called liberal values which I accepted. I knew that it was right to face up to the problems of faith, and that if you did not you only stored up trouble for the future. I knew that if you played the inquisitor with those who struggled for faith, you only revealed the insecurity of your own faith and drove them further into unbelief. In a situation of cultural pluralism where the common language of Christendom has largely broken down, "heresy" becomes a complex phenomenon. Those who chance their arm as they seek for new words and images to convey the old faith may well produce statements which sound heretical to orthodox ears, yet such pioneers may, by their personal faith and devotion, proclaim an intention to say what the Church says.

Of course good intentions are not enough, but I think it possible to be a "verbal heretic" while remaining at heart firmly orthodox. This recognition does not take away the right and duty of the Church to go on announcing what its faith is, and indeed to pass judgement on attempts to express that faith. But perhaps the recognition encourages the referee not to blow his whistle too often, to let the theological game carry on so that time is given for many follies to burn themselves out and nuggets of truth to be discerned in all manner of error. While nervous referees are forever blowing the whistle and bringing the game to a halt, those who are rather more secure allow it to proceed a little further. So I stand with liberals in believing that seekers after truth need to have their feet set in a broad room where they can move around and find their own way, in God's good time, into the fullness of his truth. This is not at all a matter of adjusting the faith to the measure of Jones's apprehension of it; it is merely the recognition that Jones will make most progress when the Church behaves with the gentleness and patience of God himself.

It was over the question of revelation that I found myself parting company with my liberal friends. I reckoned that the most terrible title given to a book of this period was *The God I Want*. If we are left to discover the god we want, we lay ourselves open to the old accusation that this god is simply the projection of our desires or, as Don Cupitt has recently said with such frankness, the name of our ideals. From my evangelical background, I had learned that the essential movement was, not from man reaching up to the skies, but from God coming down to us to declare himself. A "faith of my own" may be attractive to an élite of the naturally spiritual and thoughtful, but what of the poor, those whose energies are absorbed in the day to day task of living? If God does not come as a gift placed into empty hands then I reckoned that He was not attainable by most of the human race. The trouble is that once you insist on revelation, then you inevitably have to talk about authority and the need for our little ideas to bow the knee to ultimate truth. This worries us for we have something of a hang-up about authority. That is not without some justification for we have seen and continue to see those who say, "Thus saith the Lord", behaving in an unlovely and cruel way. We know too that authority can breed a religion of childish immaturity. So it is not surprising that modern man is called upon to be autonomous, to stand on his own feet and make his own decisions. Yet, when we have sobered down and reflected, we know that maturity is not to be equated with an adolescent rejection of authority but with the discovery of the simple fact that we depend on one another and that our fulfilment lies in a calm but critical acceptance of this interdependence. Certainly no intellectual advance is possible without building on the wisdom of others, and equally certainly this is not incompatible with the need to check and even challenge what we have received.

I suppose that, if I wanted to know the truth about Jones, I could just sit in my armchair and speculate about him, but if I did this, without any information from outside, I would have nothing more than my own picture of Jones. Because in fact I recognize that the real Jones is more than the product of my imagination, I abandon such leisurely ways and seek out the testimony of those who know Jones, and realize that there is no substitute for actually meeting Jones and allowing him to declare himself. Now it seems that for the thorough-going liberal, unwilling to trust the testimony of others, or to believe in God's self-disclosure, there is strictly speaking nothing to be said about God at all. He is hidden in the clouds of mystery and there is no break in the clouds, so that to say that God is love, is as much in doubt as to say that he is hate. We have simply no way of knowing, and are left in the situation of the one constructing a picture of Jones without information and without Jones being able to speak for himself.

In reading the Bible, it is difficult to avoid its insistence that God is the one who is free to speak for himself. This is where the issue of authority centres. I find myself opening the shortest, and earliest, gospel, that according to St Mark, and I discover even in chapter one that the puzzle of Jesus of Nazareth is a puzzle about his authority. "What is this? A new teaching! With authority he commands even the unclean spirits and they obey him" (Mark 1:27). And if I turn to an even earlier document, the First Letter of St Paul to the Thessalonians, I cannot escape the fact that the apostle speaks in a highly authoritative way. He dares to believe that the word which the Thessalonians heard from him, is not merely the word of men but really "the word of God" (1 Thessalonians 1:13). These references already take us from the authority of God to Jesus, who mediates that authority, and to chosen followers of his who seem to continue that mediation. "He who hears you hears me" (Luke 10:16). Of course the revelation of God is given, not in propositions or doctrines, but in the person of Jesus himself yet, as he lived nearly two thousand years ago, do we conclude that this revelation was only accessible to his contemporaries, leaving us with a bare record or distant memory, or is there a way in which the inaccessible mystery of God is still made tangible and real for us? Jesus, we believe, is the risen one, the living Lord, but in what ways does he now make himself available to us? Some seem to affirm that the Word made flesh has been made word again and that God is only available to us through the Bible or through doctrines, but the truth is that, before ever there was the New Testament or doctrines or creeds, there was the community of the followers of Jesus in which a whole variety of activities, preaching, praying, the celebration of sacraments, the pursuit of holiness, carried and embodied this Gospel. I was back with that picture of the Christian enterprise which my earliest study of theology had given me, a stream of life moving out from the happenings which had centred on Jesus into a variety of cultures and ages, and in which the self-disclosure of God was both carried and kept alive.

But, just as the honest observer could not but notice in

this stream the rubbish of sin, so too he might complain of the redundant lumber of past cultures, clothing which had once adorned the Gospel but now looked tattered and fit only for the jumble sale. Do we really have to carry on our shoulders all this burden of antique theology? As first-century Christians responded to Jesus in ways which were appropriate to them, why should not we do the same? But how can we get at this Jesus, to whom we wish to make our twentieth-century response, apart from those first-century ways of responding to him and communicating him?; can we remove the old clothing and discover the real Jesus? In principle some of this is possible, and we can see how critical historians have taken up the task, yet we cannot but notice that the Jesus escaping the grave-clothes of the first century tends to become adorned in nineteenth or twentieth century clothing.

But if this be the road to the real Jesus and thus to the authentic revelation of God, then it seems that the individual believer must be equipped with the skills of the historian. In fact very few of us have the time, inclination or ability to acquire such expertise, but then the only alternative is to depend on the say-so of those who have acquired it. Theologians are those who come up with the authentic picture of Jesus, and we can only hope that our preacher will communicate to us the fruit of a scholarly consensus. We should not be too sanguine, for the activity of theologians is like the activity of all scholars, never something which stands still, and it is easier to say "consensus" than to discover it. But the point is that the believer has not escaped from the problem of authority, it has simply shifted from that of Bible or Church to that of scholars. All the possibilities of being bullied by authority or of being driven into immature dependence on authority are back with us. Indeed it may seem a very odd form of authority to those who have heard the Lord say that the Gospel is hidden from the wise and revealed to babes (Luke 10:21).

While I respect the contribution of scholars to the life of the Church, they seem to me incongruous as authority figures telling us what the Christian faith is. Parish life had shown me the wisdom and insights of ordinary believers, and I was convinced that their faith, though simple, was by no means simple-minded. I found myself becoming fascinated by how people actually come to faith and are able to test the reasonableness of that faith. How had I come to faith? As this tale shows, the Gospel had been communicated to me by the Christian community through teachers, friends and above all my family. I was not a self-made Christian; I had depended on the authority of this reservoir of accumulated wisdom which worked, not by banging me on the head in a "take it or leave it" way, but by capturing my imagination. I was initially drawn by the Gospel as one is drawn by the truthfulness of a great work of art, and I gave it the assent of my heart before ever it reached my mind. But this in no way excluded the exercise of critical reason. A time came when I had to check whether what was beautiful was also true, and the main test of this was whether this vision was a hook which fitted the eye of my experience of life. Could I look the facts of life in the face, the depths of suffering in a geriatric hospital as well as the heights of a secure home life, and find that the Gospel does justice to all these facts? Did the vision ring true? I was sure that it was in ways like this that ordinary Christians come to faith and are able to test the reasonableness of that faith.

It is at this point that I ought to introduce the influence on me of John Henry Newman. I was a late-comer to his writings. In the context of nineteenth-century church history, I had found him infuriatingly distant from the social agonies of the nation. How could he have taken so seriously the petty world of university and ecclesiastical politics while Engels was writing on the condition of the English Working Classes? I was only propelled into reading his *Apologia* by the accident of dropping an altar on my toe. As well as causing much mirth in the accident department of the local hospital, and some grim satisfaction to a local dignitary who saw it as a judgement on clergymen with an itch to move altars around, it drove me into a deckchair in the vicarage garden where, dosed with aspirin to minimize the pain, I found the *Apologia* my solace. "Touchy", "over-sensitive"; all this can be said of Newman, and yet there is a grandeur in this defence of his integrity. What did his critic Charles Kingsley know of the struggle to follow conscience, avoiding illusion and only taking that one step at a time which the "kindly light" had made clear? How easy it was to sit on the touchlines passing slick judgement about whether the Vicar of St Mary's, Oxford had revealed too little of his real intentions. What did Kingsley know about that encircling gloom in which a man does not know what his intentions are, in which he hopes that his doubts are but a passing nightmare from which he will re-emerge into normality? The *Apologia* gave me a taste for Newman and I read many of his books but, above all, I loved *The Grammar of Assent*, a calm, mature book, well away from the hurly-burly of ecclesiastical controversy, and which I mention here for its vindication of the reasonableness of the faith of ordinary Christians. One of the greatest minds of the nineteenth century, rejecting intellectual élitism, was using his skills in the service of the man in the street.

The Church is a community whose common faith is a faith which ever seeks understanding. The Gospel proclaimed from our pulpits, encapsulated in creeds and dogmas or even as it comes to us in the New Testament, is the result of such faithful pondering. The old, old story of Jesus is told, but also the implications of it are drawn out and ever fresh attempts are made to articulate its meaning. St John of the Cross is, of course, right when he says: "When God gave us, as he did, his Son, who is his one Word, he spoke everything to us, once and for all in that one Word. There is nothing further for him to say." Indeed all the riches are given to us in Christ; no new revelations of God are needed. In this way a first-century Jewish Christian, who would be deeply puzzled and even offended by a later fifth-century understanding of Christ, was as much in possession of the fullness of faith as any disciple of the Council of Chalcedon, with its richer articulation of this faith. But if God has nothing further to say, the Church has and that for two good reasons.

First, because it takes time to understand any great event. The impression I get from reading the varied writings of the New Testament is that of men overwhelmed by the greatness of what had happened in Jesus and so responding to it with a riot of images and theologies. The apostolic Church had struck oil, but the moment of abundance and creativity had to be followed by the more sober task of carrying what had been discovered throughout the world. Indeed time brought, not a dwindling memory, but deeper understanding. Instant biographies are notorious for their lack of perspective, while those written at a decent distance from their subject are generally agreed to produce the more balanced portrait. We are right to trace back the flowering of these later understandings of Jesus to their seeds in earlier ones, and even to try to peer behind these to what a detached historian might accept as probable fact. Doing this we can test the links between various understandings of Jesus and look for their grounding in what may have happened. Only in this way can we avoid the "modernism" of cutting the link between the Christ of faith and the Christ of history. However, we should not thereby fall for the non sequitur that the earliest articulations of faith are more adequate than the later ones. Although the one Christ if preached by both the first-century Jewish Christian and the fifth-century Chalcedonian, yet it can be claimed that the latter at the level of articulation does more justice to the mystery of Christ than the more primitive theology of the former.

Second, the Church goes on having things to say because it moves through time and space and does not insulate itself from those cultures through which it passes. Decisive for this catholicity was the bold step it took in moving out into the Graeco-Roman world. It was a great risk, roots with its Jewish past could have been snapped, its identity submerged by the spirit of the age, and there were the nervous stay-at-homes who resisted the step. Some thought it inappropriate to use the terminology of Greek philosophy, "of the same substance", to witness to the mystery of the Son of God's relation to God the Father. But because God in Christ had risked himself in time and space, the way of faithfulness was defined as the way of risk, which drives the Church to embrace cultural variety, to engage in the endless task of shaping and moulding words and images as witnesses to the Gospel.

"Here below to live is to change, and to be perfect is to have changed often." These famous words of Newman pinpoint the fact of change and development in the life of the Church. Sometimes the doctrine of the incarnation is defended by reading back into the New Testament the fully fledged affirmation of Chalcedon, but this does less than justice to the facts. Although the seeds of the doctrine are well sown in scripture, notably in the Johannine tradition, and although that later understanding came by way of a true following of this tradition, I am bound to say that if other, equally scriptural, lines had been developed, the Church's understanding of Christ would have been Arian rather than Chalcedonian. What was involved was a genuine choice by the Church of what would be its master theme.

Now some have been so struck by the gap between the various understandings of Christians, the real changes which have taken place, that they have reduced the element of continuing identity to the bare minimum. With all these differences what makes us think that we are talking about the same enterprise and the same message? Is not the best we can say, that we are engaged in responding to Jesus of Nazareth as our forefathers were engaged? We shall not look for continuities in doctrines or forms of worship but only in the minimal recognition that Jesus of Nazareth is central to all our struggles to believe in God. This sharp sense of "the pastness of the past", and the difficulty of communication between the ages, fails to do justice to the problematic nature of all human communication. Here is Smith, one bundle of particular experiences, and here is Brown with another. They may speak the same language but they are two different worlds and, as we know, in any dialogue there is much scope for misunderstanding and missing the point. Of course the greater the difference in language, culture and background, the greater is the possibility of failure in communication. My wife and I felt this when, as benighted Southerners, we entered the very particular culture of the North-East. But none the less the miracle happens and communication does take place. Shakespeare's plays cannot be divorced from his particular age and yet, performed today before packed audiences, they evidently ring bells with us and make good sense. Although we in the twentieth century may not hear in exactly the same way what Shakespeare's contemporaries heard, we have no doubt that the voice we hear is that of the bard. London theatre-goers recently flocked to watch a cycle of mediaeval mystery plays. Despite the use of modern costume, the drama was clearly rooted in a past age with very different assumptions from our own, the framework was alien and odd, and yet the audience was deeply involved in the drama; successful communication had taken place across the ages. At least one Christian found himself saying, "Yes, this too is my faith", and doing this in a way which went beyond the vague sense that he was united with his forefathers in believing in God in the light of Jesus.

But, if there is real change and development in the life of the Church, we must recognize that this can involve deviation as much as deeper understanding. The course of the Church's history is not ever upwards and onwards into fuller faith. There is slipping back, there are mistaken judgements and moments of amnesia when old truths are forgotten. This means that the Church has a perpetual task of sifting and discrimination. Yet exactly how is this done and who does it? Certainly theologians have their part to play but, at their wisest, they have never seen themselves as divorced from the rank and file of Christian believers but rather as servants of their brothers and sisters. Indeed part of the evidence they have to work on is the accumulated experience of this community.

Before ever theologians spun words to affirm the mystery of Christ, a detached observer, the Roman Governor Pliny, had noted that Christians were a people who met to sing hymns to Jesus "as to a god". A Roman soldier noting that his mate worshipped an executed carpenter, left for posterity a mocking piece of graffitto showing his colleague kneeling in prayer before a crucified donkey. Before ever theologians got the words right or the faith was articulated in ringing dogmas, there was the faith of the people who saw that the saving God had come near in Jesus and that it was right that he should be worshipped as God. In the task of discernment, the instinct of the faithful has a crucial role to play and its dis-coveries become part of the material on which the servant theologian has to go to work. But finally someone or somebody has to take the responsibility of gathering up all this experience and thinking and to produce a judgement, the result of the interplay between people and intellec-tuals, nailing the community's colours to the mast. At the end of the day it was left to a group of rather pedestrian bishops to say: "This is our faith."

The task of discernment and articulation in the developing life of the church is thus a collective enterprise. It is not left to individuals simply to make up their own faith, or to scholars to tell the ignorant what they ought to believe or even to bishops to lay down the law, but it is a community task involving a number of roles. I had learned many good things from the Roman Catholic lay theologian, the Baron von Hügel, and one of the best was his insistence on the variety of elements which go to make up a balanced church life. He spoke of the Institutional, the Mystical and the Intellectual. It can easily be seen how this applies to our present subject, the "institutional" bishops, the spiritual or "mystical" insight of the people, and the intellectual labours of theologians. Many ecclesiastical ills, he claimed, stemmed from the malfunctioning or ignoring of one or other of these elements and, caught up as he was in the modernist witch-hunt, he had personal and painful experience of this. However he never believed that if the integrity of the functions were to be preserved all would be sweetness and light. Tension and conflict between bishops and theologians, theologians and people, were inevitable. The Church's task was not to evade conflict but to ensure that it was creative, the sort of clash from which the sparks of insight might fly.

Of course that, by itself, might suggest that the Church was an endless debating society but this is not the case, for we are encouraged to believe that such conflicts can be fruitfully resolved. The Church has the ability to make a judgement and articulate its faith. There are those who are nervous of this final stage of "definition", holding that it is an attempt to fit the mystery of God into the pint-pots of our all too human language. In fact it is simply the recognition that there is woe to the Church if it does not preach the Gospel. "How are they to believe in him whom they have never heard? And how are they to hear without a preacher?" (Romans 10:14). The Church is in business to use inadequate human words to articulate the Gospel, to say what it believes, to state its mind. Of course the words do not encapsulate the mystery, of course there is more to be said and perhaps what is said could have been said better. But the Church chances its arm in the humble belief first, that it is maintained in truth, that despite all errors it is held in the hands of the God of truth, and second, that the Holy Spirit allows it faithfully to state the Gospel so that verbal signposts are set up which can be trusted. Ignore them and you will wander off into error; take note of them and the path will open up for you into a yet more energetic search for understanding. The Church's solemn pronouncements have not blown the whistle on thought, but have set up markers pointing the way to further profitable pondering.

On such themes I was reflecting at Barnard Castle. They were not concerned with ecclesiastical frills and fancies but touched the very heart of my faith and that of those whom I served. What is involved in jumping into that stream of life and trying to share its faith? Such basic questions did, however, raise further ones about the Church of England and the Church of Rome. Did Anglicans possess the equipment to deal with this need for continuing discrimination and articulation in the developing life of the Church? If you asked the question "What is the faith of the Church of England?" who would answer your question? You would be directed to the 1662 Prayer Book and be told that it was all there for you to find. But if you objected and said that this was a dumb book which could not answer your twentieth-century questions, where then would you go – to the General Synod? To the High Court of Parliament? Perhaps you would broaden the question and ask instead "What is the faith of Anglicans?", and you might look hopefully to the

Lambeth Conference of Bishops, which every ten years manages to say a good deal, but your hopes would be dashed by the insistence that, edifying though these Conferences might be, they had no binding authority. If one looks to the gospels, Simon Peter is seen as the one who, in the name of his fellow apostles, confesses that Jesus is the Christ, the Son of God, and is given the task of confirming his brethren in their faith. While the Anglican Communion had had lots of Johannine theological explorers and sharp Pauline challengers, it did seem to have a Petrine-shaped hole, no place for the articulator of its faith.

In later years I was to hear an eminent and moderate Anglican theologian say quite bluntly: "The Anglican Communion needs the papacy to make it work." I began to suspect that this was the case and that all Christians needed the service of Peter exercised through the Bishop of Rome. I knew that you could no more read the papacy out of scripture than you could read out bishops or the doctrine of the incarnation. Just as there was in scripture that firmly sown seed of apostolicity, from which both the New Testament itself and the episcopate grew, and an understanding of Christ in St John's gospel which was to flower in the affirmation that Jesus was true God and true man, so it seemed that the same sort of relationship existed between the figure of Peter and the later developed papacy. Because the Lord of the Church is not simply the Jesus of the past in Galilee but the living Lord, both episcopate and papacy can be truly said to have been instituted by him. I began to ask myself on what grounds I accepted the episcopate and rejected the papacy, as indeed I had asked Nonconformists on what grounds they accepted the Canon of the New Testament and rejected the episcopate. All seemed to be developments which had their roots in the early Christian witness, and I could not see how one could reasonably pick and choose amongst these bits of ecclesiastical kit. Of course I was worried by the fact that the implementation of Vatican 1 by over zealous enthusiasts had left the papacy dangerously isolated from the rest of the life of the Church. That threatened what I believed to be the catholic and balanced picture of development and articulation as a communal enterprise. After all, if one took the New Testament image of Peter seriously then one had to recall that our Lord had rebuked the Prince of the Apostles for acting the part of Satan (Matthew 16:23), and had commanded him to leave the Beloved Disciple free to pursue his particular path (John 21:22). One wondered what papal zealots like Cardinal Manning really made of St Paul bluntly rebuking Peter for being wrong (Galatians 2:11). Scripture does not present the Petrine ministry as a one-man band. Yet, as I read the documents of Vatican 2, I had to admit that this imbalance had in principle been corrected; the pope was now set clearly within the context of his fellow bishops. Indeed so many of the questions which I, as a child of the Reformation, had put to the Church of Rome, seemed, in the Council documents on Revelation and the Church, to be receiving substantial answers expressed in a language to which I could respond. But this in itself raised further disturbing questions: "If so many misunderstandings were being cleared up, if I could see more and more areas of common faith and indeed one part of the ecclesiastical jig-saw which we needed and which Rome had to offer, what was still keeping us apart? What justified the separation? And were the Churches of the Reformation responding to Rome with the same rigour and warmth as Rome was responding to us?"

I suppose that, without realizing it, I was beginning to swim in the stream of catholic thought and enjoying the experience. If someone had said that I was a crypto-papist I would have been horrified, for I could never understand those in the Church of England who plundered the liturgical resources of Rome without joining that communion, but here I was actually plundering the theological resources of Rome. I simply felt at home with the ability of modern catholic theologians to handle the tradition yet to handle it creatively.

This was particularly the case with the Jesuit theologian Karl Rahner. I had originally been drawn by his essays on the theology of pastoral work and, as I began to pursue the more complex paths of his *Theological Investigations*, I noted how the priorities of pastoral care and spirituality informed all that he wrote. Hard going though Rahner often is, he is one of those great theologians who, instead of trapping his reader in the mystification of theological mumbo-jumbo, stretches the mind ever outwards towards the inaccessible mystery of God. He is thus the godliest of Christian thinkers, never shrinking God into a verbal counter to be moved around in some intellectual game. It was with his help that I was able to look afresh at some of the old stumbling-blocks which had made the dogmas of Rome seem fanciful and inaccessible. Rahner provided me with footholds on the mountain of faith, insights which made me see that what I had dismissed as nonsense could begin to make surprisingly good sense.

Thus I could glimpse that the dogma of the Assumption of Mary had to do with the truth that she, who is so identified with her Son in his humiliation that she gives her heart to be pierced, also shares in his glory. This glory is the fulfilment, not of a detached soul, but of her whole being. God does not jealously guard his glory but longs to share it with us, so that we are raised up and seated with Christ in the heavenly places (Ephesians 2:6). I even began to see that the dogma of the Immaculate Conception, far from elevating Mary out of the sphere of creaturely existence, connects with the Reformation insistence on the prevenient grace of God. Mary is not an autonomous god-like heroine, but called, chosen and equipped by God before ever she is able to respond to God.

There were puzzles still, of course, but I think that I was losing my taste for truth cut down to the size of my apprehension of it. While it was my duty to apprehend as far as I could, I reflected that, if God be God, the massive rock overwhelming me, then it would be odd if I were not a bit puzzled. Faith seeks understanding but this is the work of a life-time and beyond. Even when we see face to face, we shall still be confronted by inexhaustible mystery. All that the Church can require of the stumbling pilgrim is that he should learn to say: "I want to believe all that God has revealed of himself. It is into this truth that I want to grow. Lord, I believe, help thou mine unbelief."

I had to face the fact that a number of trails seemed to be converging on a Rome-ward path and that the time had come to share my problems with Hilary. She is always able to bring my whirling speculations down to earth and let in bracing winds of reality to blow away at least some of my illusions. We were on holiday in Wensleydale and, as it turned out, I could not have chosen a worse moment. Hilary was beginning to suspect that she was pregnant again, and naturally the prospect of her husband going out into the wilderness was particularly daunting. But, at this stage, I could honestly assure her that this Romish business was but a niggle, a suspicion. After all, there were signs that the Church of England might be able to face up to the issues which troubled me. The Anglican-Roman Catholic International Commission was not only coming up with an encouraging amount of agreement but, through its method of dialogue, was forcing both partners to state more clearly and in acceptable language where they stood. If what ARCIC stated was agreed by the Anglican Communion as a whole, then we should have found a voice which expressed our beliefs on a number of important matters. Moreover I had to recognize that theoretical difficulties could be a disguise for that restlessness which is the common lot of the middle-aged.

I was making rather heavy weather of the challenges of Barnard Castle and saw that fine ideas, posing as angels of conscience, could simply be tempting avenues of escape from the pressures. I was much helped by the spirituality of the French Jesuit Jean-Pierre de Caussade with his insistence that "the 'one thing necessary' is always to be found by the soul in the present moment". "The present moment", he taught, "is always the ambassador who declares the order of God." We often find it hard to discern this sacrament of the present moment, and escape either into nostalgia for the past or dreams for the future. I took the point and tried again to immerse myself in all the fascinations of parochial work. Ron Treasure in Hull had always taught me that when you are battered and ground down, the best thing is to go and visit a few sick and lonely parishioners.

So it would be very misleading to give the impression that my time at Barnard Castle was spent in endless brooding on theological problems. There was work to be done in which I believed and which I enjoyed. This work was greatly enhanced by having, as my colleague, Christopher Lewis, an able sociologist of religion and an extraordinarily efficient pastor. Together we not only talked and laughed about parish matters but discussed theological issues. There were still battles to be fought on behalf of the community. Our excellent primary school was in an extremely dilapidated state, with lavatories still half-open to the elements at the far end of the playground. As chairman of the managers, I found myself leading a campaign for school lavatories which was exactly what was needed to keep my feet on the ground. It was to broaden into a struggle for the whole future of the school, and for proper consultation with teachers and parents in the formulation of these plans. I find myself irritated with bureaucracies, whether secular or ecclesiastical, when they treat with contempt those on the spot who have to live with the results of their decision-making and who actually know most about the situation in question. Of course officials must set local problems in a wider context, but they can only do this in an acceptable way if they learn the art of genuine consultation. A model display of this important art was given by our local M.P., Jim Boyden, when he came, at my invitation, to attend a meeting of parents. During our short stay in Barnard Castle we had no less than two General Elections. I had lost none of that passion for elections which had begun at school and I know no greater pleasure than sitting up all night, fortified with a few bottles of beer and some pork pies, to watch the results come in. Some of the fun has been taken out of it by those maddeningly correct computer predictions, and one only hopes that in the future, three-party races will restore some element of surprise. On the more serious side I enjoyed chairing pre-election meetings at which all the candidates appeared on one platform in our church hall. The politicians played to packed houses, and I am glad to say that ecclesiastical sponsorship did not damp down enthusiasm or quell the vigorous heckling.

SIX

Oxford

In 1975 an old friend, Ronald Gordon, then Vicar of the University Church of St Mary's in Oxford, was appointed Bishop of Portsmouth. It is one of the peculiarities of the establishment that following such episcopal appointments, the patronage of the parish being vacated falls, on this occasion, to the Crown. The invitation I received to succeed Ronald Gordon thus came from 10 Downing Street, causing friends who knew my views on establishment a good deal of genial laughter. Having consulted trusted advisers, and encouraged by Kenneth Woollcombe, then Bishop of Oxford, I accepted the invitation. When I became a Roman Catholic, a parishioner posed a sharp but justifiable question: if I was already suffering from a Romish niggle, had I been really honest in accepting the post? All I can say is that the niggle, at that time, was still only a cloud which I expected to pass. Maybe at Barnard Castle I had been a square peg in a round hole, and the challenge of a new and very different job might be exactly what was needed to settle me back in my Anglicanism.

Perhaps it was dangerous to trust myself to the ambience of that former vicar turned Roman Catholic, John Henry Newman. As I was to discover, you do not need much sensitivity to be aware of his presence in that lovely building. Kneeling up in the chancel after the daily evening prayer, I was to find myself quite naturally asking for the prayers of this fellow pilgrim, but it was a reassuring rather than a disturbing presence, especially when, in the early hours of a Sunday morning, I would celebrate the old Prayer Book order of Holy Communion. It was this same liturgy, these same words, which were the roots from which had sprung that rich crop of parochial sermons which this saintly predecessor had preached. But St Mary's was the church, not only of Newman, but of Russell Barry, George Cockin (whose archdeacon my father had been), Dick Milford and Roy Lee, all men of a more liberal persuasion. St Mary's was thus the meeting place of many different streams of Anglican life, and I saw in this fact a clue as to what I should try to do as vicar. Here were streams of affirmation – Newman hot on dogma – and streams of free enquiry – a long tradition of St Mary's as a thinking person's church, the place where the University's motto "The Lord my Light" was celebrated, almost every Sunday in term, by a University sermon.

As I have already shown, I was struggling to see how a belief in God's revelation could be reconciled with liberal values, how the truth boldly announced could yet be a truth which sets free, and it seemed that St Mary's provided a wonderful opportunity to engage with a congregation in the practical working out of this. While honouring the University Church's vigorous intellectual tradition, I confess that I found its rather colourless worship depressing. Could not the imagination and the senses be captured as well as the mind? I had never much liked the ecclesiastical parties of the Church of England, but did not believe that a decent moderate mid-point between extremes was the answer. "Central Churchmanship", with its Laodicean overtones of being neither hot nor cold, was really something less than the bold attempt to comprehend and embrace the best of all worlds. However, as Ronald Gordon had already improved the quality of St Mary's worship and established a eucharistically centred framework, I would not have to arrive as an innovator, but as the developer of a way already pioneered.

I did not realize how difficult it would be to appeal to the minds of students. The university world is very volatile and it is all too easy to return to it lumbered with a view of it which is already out of date. Where once there had been revolution, fierce questioning and long hair, there was now a notable air of conformity, sports jackets and short back and sides. The economic climate means that graduates are no longer welcomed into jobs with open arms, and this encourages a single-minded attention to getting a good degree and some sort of niche in the outside world. The present generation of students is hard-working and tends to lend a more willing ear to religion than to politics. Unlike my Sunday-school-educated generation, they know little about Christianity and so come to it with freshness and zeal. Evangelicals have weighed up the situation with great care and efficiently manage to provide the simple basics of the faith but, if they are good at Christian initiation, they are less good at the business of growth and development. Because they allow too little room for the mind to awaken to questioning, problems are swept under the carpet only to emerge later to threaten the structure of an over-simplified and too neatly packaged faith. There seemed to be a place for St Mary's to provide something which was lacking. I was determined that what we did should supplement and not rival the solid work being done in the colleges by the chaplains. The real parish churches of the University are the college chapels, and it is there that the bread and butter of pastoral work gets done. St Mary's was not in business to cream off religious enthusiasm into yet another ecclesiastical empire but to support and supplement this work.

As I considered the history of St Mary's I perceived another clear task. It is a church scarred by the wounds of Christian disunity. Many know that Thomas Cranmer passed from it to his martyrdom, but fewer know that a little later a former vicar, Stephen Rousham, was to be martyred as a recusant priest in Gloucester. Not only was Newman a man despised and rejected by the establishment, ecclesiastical and university, but so before him was another eminent preacher from that pulpit, John Wesley. A church sad with the pain of Christian division, surely had a particular vocation to be an agent of reconciliation.

Through its connection with the Student Christian Movement, St Mary's had for long been engaged in this work, but with the Movement's collapse, I believed that, rather than attempting to revive it, we should find new ways of doing a similar task. As well as making sure that we had a regular flow of Free Church and Roman Catholic preachers, I was glad of opportunities to provide a home for various ecumenical occasions, whether it was Bruce Kent or Trevor Huddleston preaching on peace and justice, the German Lutheran congregation continuing that connection with St Mary's which had begun in the dark days of 1939, or the Jesuits celebrating the four hundredth anniversary of the martyrdom of Edmund Campion. It was important to keep the doors open for such events. The only time we kept them closed was when Ian Paisley and his followers demonstrated against the papal visit by marching from St Mary's to the Broad Street, "in the steps of the Oxford martyrs". That was an instructive occasion. Mild old ladies and quiet little men sat around in the Radcliffe Square drinking tea and munching sandwiches. They could have been on any parish outing. Then suddenly away went the Thermos flasks and out came the banners carrying their scurrilous messages: "The blasphemous fable of the Mass" – "Judas got his thirty pieces – what have you got, Runcie?" It was the eruption of hatred out of such apparent normality which seemed so shocking. We were given a salutary reminder, not only that English anti-popery is not wholly dead, but that such violent hatred can boil up in the most ordinary of people. When rebuked by one of Mr Paisley's followers for shutting him out of St Mary's, I could only reply: "Our doors are open to all except those who hate."

Special ecumenical services could only provide the public face of our work and something more solid needed to happen behind the scenes. In Oxford, as in Barnard Castle, early enthusiasm for unity had waned, leaving a thin red line of activists. Everyone wanted friendly relations with other Christians, but when it came to leaving the home ground to worship away in another church, few seemed willing to make the effort. There was not much zeal for risking old accustomed ways in the death of our separate denominations to rise to the new life of unity. Yet, over the years, we did see a few solid bridges built and the first steps made in establishing an enduring relationship between St Mary's and the great Methodist Wesley Memorial Church.

As always there was a gulf between the vision and its realization. I lack the imagination and drive to be an achiever, and I suppose that my own private questioning somewhat sapped the confidence necessary for the task. But God works through our failures and I believe he allowed me to do things which otherwise I could not have done. Being myself a seeker, conscious of wrestling with God, helped me to understand what other pilgrims in faith were feeling, and certainly I found great satisfaction in being allowed to help individuals to discover where God was leading them. Engaged in this sort of work, you learn the importance of allowing God to set the pace so that this unique person before you can find the particular way in which he or she is being shaped by God. Saints do not pour off a conveyor belt all looking the same, mass produced, but are hand-made by the Divine Craftsman. Because St Mary's has such a tiny geographical parish and because its role is so very unclear, it provides opportunities for a priest to engage in such personal and rewarding work. If you leave yourself around and try to give the impression of being leisured, a surprising number of people will come to talk about their problems and their search for faith.

Whatever successes or failures there were, St Mary's was a joy and a delight. I could not have been surrounded by more congenial clerical and lay colleagues. Each assistant priest made his own distinctive contribution: David Whittington, gifted as musician and motor mechanic, Tim Gorringe, a well-read disciple of Karl Barth, Peter Allen, whose gifts of spiritual counsel have now led him to become a monk at Mirfield, and finally Chris Foster and Ralph Townsend, whose friendship and advice meant so much to me in those last difficult months at St Mary's. They carried burdens heavier than any vicar should expect his assistants to carry. But St Mary's is essentially a lay person's church. Priests come and go but the continuity is provided by the laity, who not only carry the responsibility of keeping the show going, but are always fertile with new ideas for moving forward.

As vicar I enjoyed the support and friendship of a remarkable line of churchwardens. They soon perceived the frailty of my administrative ability. That was a problem, for St Mary's has always been a centre for events both sacred and secular, and in recent years has had to cope, not only with the usual mixture of concerts, memorial services and plays, but also with many thousands of overseas visitors. Some organizational ability is needed, and mercifully we were able to afford a lay administrator who took out of my hands many tasks at which I was frankly incompetent. A similar shift of responsibility took place in the control of Parochial Church Council meetings. Oxford is a great place for committees, and there seems to be an insatiable thirst for participation in decision-making. However little expertise one can muster on a given subject, it is yet judged to be a solemn duty to have and express a view. As every issue has to be approached from every angle and all possible objections scrutinized, the process, while admirably fair and thorough, does not make for decisiveness, and even when a decision has been reached, the charming humility of academics goes on questioning whether it has been the right one. Thus Oxford committees tend to go on circling round and round one issue. I was to discover that I approached meetings of the P.C.C. with an apprehension similar to that confessed by heads of Colleges at meetings of their governing bodies. Unlike them I was rescued by the wise decision that I should normally vacate the chair to allow my competent churchwardens to take over, while I retired to the more congenial back benches. In this atmosphere, where lay responsibility was taken for granted and we were not fussed by demarcation disputes, it was easy to introduce both men and women to the liturgical role of assisting in the distribution of the Holy Communion.

This lay ministry went much further than just keeping St Mary's going. In all the churches where I have served, I have been conscious of those with demanding and responsible jobs whose lay vocations would suffer if, as one put it, they were too deeply "sucked into the vortex of church life". Faithful in their worship, Sunday by Sunday, they come to be serviced for that real ministry which takes place in the secular world. We needed to make it clear that this life of the Church, dispersed and hidden in the world, was every bit as much "church life" as all the good things which went on in and around St Mary's. The "gathered" Church can become self-indulgent and parasitic on the Christian mission if it extracts too much time and energy from its members. Of course the life of common worship, shared faith and mutual support is important, and it needs the unselfish labours of many, but we had to get the balance right so that the people of God, instead of being imprisoned in an ecclesiastical ghetto, were set free for their properly secular work. Although I suppose that we never got the mixture right, we were able to articulate the problem and begin to work on its solution.

Ministry at St Mary's was absorbing, but the old niggle was still there and getting at me in a number of ways. In 1977 a book of essays, *The Myth of God Incarnate*, was published. The general argument of its authors ran something like this: the language of incarnation, of Jesus being the second "person" of the Holy Trinity living a human life, is not "literal" but mythological or poetical, a way of expressing his continued significance for us in our search for God. The contributors, with varying degrees of strength, argued that this "myth" is no longer useful and appropriate. John Hick saw it as a barrier to understanding the work of God in other world religions. It made Christianity parochial and exclusive. Don Cupitt believed that it fatally distorted the real meaning of Jesus and compromised the transcendence of God. Reviewing the book in our parish paper, I detected a difference of emphasis amongst its authors. Maurice Wiles, our Regius Professor of Divinity, took a softer line towards "myth" and its articulation in creeds, Christmas cribs and carols, arguing that as long as it was not understood as "literal" language, these could remain living ways of expressing the centrality of Jesus. But Hick and Cupitt were sharper. For them the "myth" was mischievous, and being so logically required a more radical uprooting of its expression in popular devotion. If Cupitt were right, that the worship of Jesus is "a paganization of Christianity", then truth demanded that we should no longer be encouraged to kneel before the Christmas crib or merrily carol the idolatrous words "come let us adore him". Michael Goulder and Don Cupitt attempted to dig behind the language of incarnation to Jesus as he is discoverable by an historian. Goulder came up with "the Man of Universal Destiny", and Cupitt with the "Witty Rabbi". Dennis Nineham, having no such confidence in the rediscovery of the Jesus of history, took a very different line. He questioned whether it was worthwhile to attempt to trace the Christian's everchanging understanding of his relationship with God back to some identifiable life, character and activity of Jesus of Nazareth. He asked whether it is necessary "to believe in Jesus in any sense beyond that which sees him as the main figure through whom God launched man into a relationship with himself so full and rich, that, under various understandings and formulations of it, it has been and continues to be, the salvation of a large proportion of the human race." Thus to thust Jesus into the dim mists of the past is to make any relationship between him and believers problematic, and involves substituting the personal focus of traditional Christianity with a set of ideas. Although it saddened me when Goulder and Cupitt later announced that they no longer believed in the objective reality of God, I cannot say that it surprised me. For having broken the connection between Jesus of Nazareth and the transcendent God, one is left with an unknowable God who soon begins to look remarkably like no God at all.

While defending the right of such scholars of integrity to say what they believed to be true, I saw this as a thrust at the heart of Christianity. "Where", I asked in my review, "does the development of Christian doctrine end and a new religion begin?" In my judgement this book had produced a form of Christianity so unlike what we had been led to believe it to be, that it was misleading to call it the same thing. My old questioning about development, and the distinction between a deeper understanding of the riches of Christ and a deviation from this understanding, was focused sharply. What should we now think of Chalcedon's affirmation of Jesus Christ, "true God and true Man"? Was this just one of the many "everchanging understandings" of the Christian's relationship with God, something which could be jettisoned, or was it a signpost of continuing significance? Should our understanding of Jesus now depend on the latest discoveries and insights of some scholars?

Much later in my time at St Mary's, similar questions were aroused by the more notorious but less radical "David Jenkins" affair. The Bishop of Durham had been crudely reported, and fanatical critics were ascribing to him views which he certainly has never held. The tale put about by certain raucous Conservative Members of Parliament, that the Bishop denies the incarnation of the Son of God, is simply untrue; he has in fact been the most stalwart upholder of Chalcedonian orthodoxy.

However, while rejecting such distortions, I did think that what he had actually said raised a number of important issues and I preached a course of sermons on them. While happy to speak of Mary as "mother of God" the Bishop was unhappy about speaking of her as "the blessed Virgin". While rejoicing that Christ is truly risen from the dead, the Bishop did not think that this necessarily involved an empty tomb. He did not deny that these stories of the virginal conception and the empty tomb were of the greatest importance but questioned the relevance of their "literal" truth. Were these happenings or were they stories made up to illustrate the meaning of Jesus? Now I would agree that there are some things in the gospels about which I would say that it does not really matter whether they happened or not. Thus I have no sleepless nights over whether, when the disciples were dispatched to find money in the fish's mouth, they actually found any (Matthew 17:27). Here nothing of significance depends on whether what is alleged to have happened really happened. But equally there are other alleged events which need to have happened if what Christians profess be true. At least Jesus must have been a man who lived and who died. There are points where the Christian story has to be "fact"; "the Word" has to be "made flesh". I wondered on what grounds one felt free to shift some of the alleged happenings into the world of instructive stories and not others, and I wondered whether in doing this shifting we were still saying the same thing.

It is to be noted that David Jenkins did not base his rejection of the Virginal Conception on critical grounds, i.e. that a detached historian would not accept the testimony of St Luke as evidence for what had actually happened, but on the more general grounds that this was not, he believed, the way God acted. The implication is that God always acts in and through the regular ordering of nature and not in what is called a supernatural way. But is that the case? In one sermon I claimed that the real issue was:

> What sort of world do we live in? Is it an enclosed world for which there are no possibilities beyond the regularities of nature and the operations of the laws of the market? Such closed worlds will allow, and even value, belief in God, but God held at a distance. He cannot be the one who touches this earth. Spirituality and politics are thus sealed into separate containers. We can come to Holy Communion, eat bread and drink wine, allow our thoughts to soar to heaven, but never allow that the bread and wine could be transfigured into expressions of God's life. Now faith in the incarnation faces the facts, whether of the regularities of nature, the arms race or market forces, but it also faces events which blow a hole in these vicious circles. The Virginal Conception, the Empty Tomb challenge the closed world, affirm a world open to the infinite possibilities of God, yes even through death.

What I was struggling to say was that these "supernatural"

events showed God's freedom to cut into and make a difference in this world of flesh and blood. We were back to an old disagreement about divine grace. This grace, I believed, was not simply God's acceptance of the way things are but the new creation at work amidst the old. Certainly you can read the Annunciation and the Resurrection as stories of God's initiative in the life of Jesus and his triumph over death, but something more is added when you go on to say that these are points where the story becomes fact. New possibilities are offered to sensual earth-bound bags of bones such as we are. In fact I could not see how the Bishop of Durham's admirable care for the social problems of his people and these theological views added up. In the former I heard him insisting that there were realities beyond the realities of the market, the very reality of God which does not hover in the air as a beautiful story or fine ideal but has been made flesh in such a world as this. The Christian goes on struggling for justice and the equal value of persons, not because he is an obstinate visionary who ignores hard facts, but because in Jesus he has perceived that a more real reality has savingly impinged upon this world. While the Bishop's welcome political interventions seemed to imply such a theology, his recently expressed views on the Virginal Conception and Empty Tomb seemed to push his theology away into the realm of mere ideas and ideals.

The issues raised by *The Myth of God Incarnate* and the "Durham affair" seemed important and worth talking about, certainly not to be parodied and screamed at nor to be lightly laughed off in a bland establishmentarian way. I had no stomach for the hounding and persecuting of scholars, for their researches raised real questions, but I did believe that the Church of England ought corporately to try to answer them. It needed at least to tell the ordinary Christian whether or not he was being an idolater in singing "come, let us adore him", and to tell the preacher what there was to be said on Lady Day and Easter morning. Individuals expressed individual views but the Church of England as a whole seemed uncomfortable at the prospect of stating a corporate view and telling potential voters what was in its manifesto. The Doctrine Commission had produced two reports of great interest. In them were tackled the questions about how we believe and the context in which we believe, but the issue of what we believe was studiously avoided. Indeed, at times this silence was seen as a great Anglican virtue. Unlike cruder folk we avoided the terrible business of "defining" faith and wisely left it to be articulated in our liturgy. It was rather as if the Conservative Party left voters to deduce its manifesto from the singing of "Land of Hope and Glory" at the Party Conference. Of course it is important to show that believing and praying go together and it is indeed a fact that we learn more of faith in doing the liturgy than in poring over conciliar definitions. And yet this insight will not let us off the hook of using albeit inadequate words to express our common belief. Those of us who had sat through the Synodical debates on the Alternative Service Book, knew well that there were critical points where what went in or was left out depended on who won a particular doctrinal argument. In any case, as I have insisted before, Christianity is fundamentally a religion of articulation, of communication which springs from the very heart of God himself. By keeping silence, the Church of England gave the impression that it did not have a corporate faith but was content simply to provide a framework in which individuals could make up a faith of their own.

Yet this reluctance to articulate faith and make judgements in doctrinal disputes came at the same time as the ARCIC report on Authority was affirming the Church's duty to do exactly that. The Christian community, it was stated, is given the capacity to assess its faith and life and to speak to the world in the name of Christ. Shared commitment and belief create a common mind in determining how the Gospel should be interpreted and obeyed . . . In its mission to proclaim and safeguard the Gospel, the Church has the obligation and competence to make declarations in matters of faith.

Indeed the report went on,

at times there is conflict and debate. When conflict endangers unity or threatens to distort the Gospel, the Church must have effective means for resolving it.

Nor did the report believe that the Church was without such "effective means".

Bishops have a special responsibility for promoting truth and discerning error. They are collectively responsible for defending and interpreting the apostolic faith.

Whatever hesitations the Anglican members of the Commission continued to have about the role of the papacy, they were in complete agreement with their Roman Catholic partners in holding that the authority of God is exercised through the service of authority in the Church, which is not that of scholars but of bishops.

There is always a gap between the theory of ecumenical documents and ecclesiastical realities. So Anglicans gently chide Roman Catholics for talking about collegiality and decentralization but being slow to deliver the goods. Now it seemed that Anglicans were talking big about authority but, confronted by an actual doctrinal dispute, were not translating theory into practice. The biggest test for Anglicanism will be to discover whether the views of its representatives on ARCIC accurately register its common mind on authority. Already this document is under fire, not only from some evangelicals but from more liberal men of the middle. Indeed evangelicals have no trouble with authority itself but only with the way it is mediated through the ministry of the Church. The liberal objection is more fundamental, for it springs from doubt as to whether the Church can authoritatively confront us with the very word of God. If the ARCIC documents showed exciting and hopeful convergence, then there was evidence that some forces of divergence were still at work. The practice of the Church of England, faced with doctrinal dispute, seemed more nearly to express the views of this critical liberal middle than those of its ARCIC representatives.

I was to detect divergence again in the proposal that the Churches in England should enter into a covenant for unity. This proposal emerged from the gloom and guilt into which we had been plunged by the failure of the Anglican/Methodist Unity Scheme. Something, it was felt, had to be done, and if plans for full organic unity had failed, perhaps a more modest proposal for a slower growth into visible unity might succeed. If we could accept one another as full members of the Body of Christ and one another's ministries as full ministries in the Church, although we might not end our separations we could enter into a situation of full intercommunion. I was in a great dilemma for I too mourned the failure of the Anglican/Methodist scheme, yet the new proposals seemed weak exactly where the old ones had been strong. While we had laboured with Methodists in serious doctrinal dialogue, the new approach, in its brisk pragmatism, seemed to sweep differences under the carpet. While the old scheme had headed for the clear goal of organic unity, the death of our separate churches, the new approach went no further than encouraging better relations between neighbours. We were in danger of being like those couples who get engaged without any clear intention of getting married. The outcome could be an acceptance of a federation of churches in which it would be all too easy to rest. When it is said that our divisions are a scandal to the world, I believe that it is truer to say they are scandalous only to those who perceive the incongruity and sinfulness of the family's inability to be gathered around the one table of the Lord. Most outsiders simply do not have this perception. To them it is our intolerance and arguments which are scandalous but not this variety of bodies representing a variety of Christian experience. Indeed our society is schooled to accept and welcome such pluralism. We have turned from the good fellowship but limitations of the old corner shop, to enjoy the greater variety offered by the supermarket where we can wander about and select according to taste. This consumer mentality has shaped our understanding of religions and values. We no longer expect one dominating religion or set of values; we like to be free to shop around. This means that a number of Churches, accepting each other's right to exist and living in peace and harmony, as the Covenanting proposals sought, would fit more nearly the requirements of an age which expects an à la carte menu of religious experience.

If the spirit of the age is reshaping the ecumenical goal, it is much assisted by Christians overcome by sheer weariness in the pursuit of unity. With so many hopes raised and then dashed, it is not surprising that even the most ardent begin to question whether we have been after the right goal. Might it not be that the rich variety of Christian experience, contained in our several denominations, would fail to survive being lumped together in one great Church? Would not something of the particular style and flavour of each Church be lost? Given the fact that divisions have often arisen in the past through the failure of mainstream Christianity to contain a wide enough variety, would not the great Church of the future inevitably prove tyrannical with the same divisive results? These are serious questions to which the new model of a federation of churches seems a reasonable answer. Moreover it can be supported by a theology of ecclesiastical pluralism grounded in the pluralism of the New Testament. In the earliest Church, it is argued, variety was the spice of life. Here was not one form of ministry or style of doctrine but many. If we can speak of a Pauline or Johannine styled Church, does this not offer us a model of unity better adapted to preserving Christian variety than the more monochrome, organically-united Church which followed? That this view now receives the weightiest support in the Church of England can be seen in the Archbishop of York's book *Church and Nation in a Secular Age*. Unity, he warns, "can increase the power of those who are already powerful, and threaten those whose contribution to the common pool could easily be submerged" (p. 149). He sees no recipe for a single united Church "at least not in the foreseeable future . . . the only practicable way forward would seem to be to acknowledge a variety of Christian identities, to accept a degree of pluralism as inevitable, indeed desirable, and to try to contain it within an overall theological understanding which gives value to the differences, without encouraging a supermarket mentality" (p. 155).

Now, while I wish to affirm the importance of variety in the life of the Church and see how this can be endangered by ecclesiastical totalitarianism, I believe that this new view of Christian unity fails to do justice to the challenge and opportunity of ecumenism. I grant that, if the Church exists simply to provide a framework in which individuals discover a faith of their own, then there is a strong argument for a variety of frameworks to suit a variety of temperaments but, once we recognize that the centre of Christianity is, not our words or thoughts about God, but

God's Word to us, then the Church as one communion and fellowship is necessary.

I confess that I find the argument from the pluralism of the New Testament to denominational federalism curiously fundamentalist and antiquarian. While ignoring the facts that St Paul argues very precisely against believers assembling on the basis of their chosen style of theology (1 Corinthians 1), and that early Christians were not presented on the Lord's Day with a choice of whether they would attend a Pauline, Johannine or Petrine church, this view implies that Christians fell away from primitive comprehensiveness into a later narrowing and exclusiveness. Surely the reverse was the case, for as the Church moved out from the womb of Judaism into the Graeco-Roman world, it was challenged to take on board yet greater variety. Because there was the risk that Christian identity would be lost, bands of unity as tough as the written New Testament, a unified ministry and the creeds, were necessary for this very task of greater comprehensiveness. What is sometimes called "primitive catholicism", with its institutionalizing of Christianity, far from constituting a narrowing of the Gospel, provided the means whereby that Gospel, in its integrity, could plunder the wealth of the Gentiles. A consideration of what came to be recognized as the authoritative writings of the New Testament shows what organic unity is all about. Instead of presenting us with an à la carte menu of religious experience, inviting us to select – "I for Paul", "I for Mark", and "I for John" – in its rich variety it offers us a balanced diet and invites us to accept all. I may be initially drawn by the Johannine tradition which sits lightly to institutions, but then what I need is a dash of the witness of the Pastoral Epistles, which will help me see how this religion of the spirit has to be incarnated in institutions. So, the New Testament variety exists, not to be parcelled out in separate sectarian containers, but to be held together for our enrichment and completeness as balanced Christians. All things are to be ours.

To hold ever more variety in one communion and fellowship is a humanly impossible task; just how impossible it is we see when we turn to the secular scene. Every news bulletin contains yet more evidence of the forces which divide. Nationalism burgeons, and the fragile bonds we have forged to hold us together – the rule of international law and the United Nations – are treated with contempt in the name of our various understandings of "national interest". But, as we go our own way and ruthlessly seek our own interests, we know that this planet is too small to permit the free-for-all of every country for itself. Unless we learn to live together, we shall die together. If we look at South Africa we know that cultural apartheid, the attempt to allow variety to develop in separate containers, simply does not work. If we look no further than our own doorsteps, Toxteth or Handsworth, the perils of neglecting national unity are clear. There is simply no realistic alternative but to rediscover human variety as the way of mutual enrichment rather than the cause of division. It is in this broad context that I have always seen the urgent need for Christian unity and it is this context which should now sharpen our resolve to go for the impossible, sustained by the conviction that, amongst our human divisiveness, the Holy Spirit of convergence lives and is at work. Keeping on course for the goal of organic unity is a matter of more than ecclesiastical interest, it is necessary if we are to fulfil our calling to offer hope to a despairing world. The Church, said Vatican 2, "is in the nature of a sacrament – a sign and instrument of communion with God and of unity among men".

Believing that the covenanting plan was luring us away from this high calling, I felt obliged, with heavy heart, to oppose it. Here again I was forced to see that, amidst the wonderful evidence of Christian convergence, there were also signs of divergence. We could not ignore them. When we all said "yes" to Christian unity, were we saying "yes" to the same thing? There seemed to be an underlying disagreement about the nature of unity, and I wondered how we could make genuine progress if we were not heading for the same goal.

The same problem emerged in the campaign for the ordination of women in the Anglican Communion, for here too convergence was threatened by an act of divergence. On the substantial issue of whether women can be ordained or not, I was and am undecided. It seems to me clear that God is calling us to take more seriously the vocation of women in the Church, but I am not clear whether this is a summons to ordain women or to discover other distinctive forms of ministry for them. If our main concern is to rediscover the feminine in the Church, then it could be that the ordination of women would turn out to be an imprisonment in a male mould. But the truth of the matter can only be got at by seeking to discern what God may be saying to us in the feminist movement, and for this to be done successfully we need an essentially intercultural study whereby our various biases can be checked. For, whether we be Orthodox Greeks stubbornly opposed to the ordination of women, or North Americans wildly in favour, we are all unconscious prisoners of our culture. To get at the truth we need, not independent action, but interdependence, a careful thinking together.

As far as arguments for or against are concerned, they seem to me largely unimpressive. When those against assert that the priest, as an Ikon of Christ, has to be male, I cannot but recall that St Paul in 2 Corinthians 3:18 is referring not to ministerial priests but the whole People of God, made up of course of male and female. When those in favour speak of the lopsidedness of an all-male priesthood, and argue that women are needed for the completeness of ministry, I note that our great High

Priest is male and wonder whether his priesthood is therefore thought to be incomplete. However, I was concerned with the understanding of the Church and its unity which this proposal seemed to reflect, and found myself questioning whether a national Church could decide by itself to ordain women. I had the greatest difficulty in persuading Anglicans that this was other than a legalistic point. When I was ordained in York Minster, I was told firmly that I was ordained priest in the Church of God, not just in the Church of England, indeed that there was no such thing as an Anglican ministry. Far from being a point of minute ecclesiastical detail, this assertion is fundamental to an understanding of the English Reformation. At that time, the Church of England, so hot for the freedom of the local church to go its own way, broke with the papacy, yet took some care to preserve other bonds which tied it into the universal Church. Canon of scripture, the gospel sacraments, the creeds and, according to the Preface to the Ordinal, the three-fold ministry, were seen as such. The Church of England, for all its independence, continued to claim a share in that divine property which had been entrusted to the universal Church. It was surely difficult to take this seriously if we treated the sensitive and important issue of the ordination of women as a matter for unilateral action. Denials that this was a fundamental issue did not ring true in the light of assertions that through the ordination of women an incomplete ministry would become complete.

I could not see how the Church of England could have it both ways. If its ministry was but a share in divine property committed to the universal Church, then it had to behave accordingly. However right the action in itself might seem to be, it was not right to act alone. It would be as if horticultural enthusiasts decided to dig up common land, the village green, and plant onions, believing that this was a better use for it than all the activities of children on their swings and roundabouts, and of sportsmen with their cricket and football. They might have been right but they did not have the right to behave with what had been entrusted to all as if it were their own. When I came out of St Mary's and was approached by a man wanting a few shillings for a meal, I was at liberty to dig into my own pocket but not, without permission, to dispense the church collection. At the heart of the debate on the ordination of women I saw a conflict between ecclesiastical nationalism and internationalism, between autonomy and interdependence. Of course this touched the raw nerve of the English Reformation. I found myself quoting the words of Thomas More:

> This realm, being but one member and small part of the Church, might not make a particular law disagreeable with the general law of Christ's Universal Catholic Church, no more than the City of London, being but one poor member in respect of the whole realm, might make a law against an Act of Parliament to bind the whole nation.

Of course, as I quoted these words against what I took to be a reassertion of the independence of the national Church, I was aware that they had been spoken against Henry VIII's original assertion of independence from the papacy. Indeed, when in 1984 the General Synod voted to set in motion the machinery to implement the ordination of women, it was celebrating almost exactly the four hundred and fiftieth anniversary of Henry's Act of Supremacy. Certainly it is true that many good things have happened in the Church because the few have taken an initiative and then the institutional elephant has come lumbering afterwards but it is alas also true that the pursuit of good things, at all costs, has been one of the causes of our unhappy divisions. Did we really want a re-run of the mistakes of the Reformation? Had we not begun to see that acting together was a surer way to renewal?

But, if I could detect forces of divergence in Anglicanism, were they not also at work in the Roman Communion? The Bishop of Birmingham, Hugh Montefiore, had accused some Anglicans of having a romantic love affair with Rome. There is, of course, truth in this, for what leads an individual into Catholic unity is not simply rational argument. As in so many discoveries, the heart and imagination are captured first and the mind follows. So, in all honesty, I must admit that in my pilgrimage, I felt the attractiveness of the Roman communion in a multitude of small ways. Years ago I had discovered that catholic churches were good places to pray in, for somehow they communicated to me both the mystery of God and his homeliness. I had a particular fondness for Westminster Cathedral with its holy busyness. Again I admired the way in which the Catholic Church, providing a home for souls as diverse as Alec Guinness, Karl Rahner and Diana Dors, ministered to a wide range of temperaments and classes. Such impressions do capture the heart and I have no quarrel with these being seen as evidence of a love affair. Indeed it seems that "having a love affair" is a better model for ecumenical aspiration than that of the merger of two industrial companies. Surely Anglicans ought to fall in love with Rome and Roman Catholics with Canterbury. This is the right language to describe the marriage of our Churches. But of course we do not enter into marriage unadvisedly, lightly or wantonly, seeing our potential partner through rose-tinted spectacles. Perhaps that is what the Bishop of Birmingham was getting at.

While seeing so many difficulties in my own beloved Church was I blinded by a romantic haze to the faults of Rome? I was concerned and remain concerned about the security of intellectual freedom in the Church of Rome, for I had read a good deal about the suppression of the so-called Modernist movement and I did not much like what I saw. That orgy of spying and tale-telling was both dis-tasteful and wasteful of much talent. Given wiser and more generous pastoral care, a George Tyrrell, with his enormous theological creativity, instead of being cruelly excommunicated could have given much to the Catholic Church. While recognizing the right of the Church to judge whether this or that teacher is actually teaching the faith of the Church, I believed that more Christ-like methods would have retained for the Church his great gifts and given him the balance which his soul required.

Vatican 2, and the burst of theological energy which followed it, seemed to show that the Church had learned its lesson. Overnight suspect theologians like de Lubac and Congar became respectable and accepted. It was inevitable that, as the new spirit of freedom allowed a backlog of thought to burst forth, mud as well as clear water would emerge. It was also natural that cautious souls would become nervous at what had been let out of the bag and would try to fit the toothpaste back into the tube. The treatment of Küng, Schillebeeckx and Boff, although mild by earlier standards, did show a failure in genuine dialogue and communication between authority and such pioneering theologians. To the fairminded observer the Roman Catholic Church does not look like a community in which the mind has been suppressed, for the fertility and variety of its theology is pretty impressive. One has to admit though that the task of holding together such creativity and the continuing affirmation of the Church's faith is a difficult one. Where scholars advance from being virtuoso soloists to making their distinctive contribution to the Church's orchestra, some disciplines are required but the results are richer. The catholic biblical scholar Raymond Brown is realistic about the problems and tensions involved, but is able to affirm: "I would rather live in a Church where authorities can get excited and worried over what theologians are saying, even to the point of chastising them, than in a Church which ignores them" (*The Critical Meaning of the Bible*, p. 122). What may not yet be fully grasped is that the Church of Rome is so equipped with checks and balances that no one can really mistake the wilder views of way-out theologians for the official teaching of the Church and that, thus equipped, it can afford to be more relaxed, knowing that burgeoning life, albeit a little chaotic, is better than the well-ordered tombstones of a municipal cemetery.

Whether Rome could handle intellectual ferment was but part of the wider question of whether it could provide a home for all that variety of Christian experience which had been fostered by separate denominations. If there really was a post-conciliar loss of nerve and an anxious desire to tighten things up then the prospects for such comprehensiveness were dim. Of course I had met Roman Catholics consumed by a nostalgia for the old secure fortress with its clear, sharply edged teaching and "unchanging" liturgy. They were remarkably like those members of the Church of England who hankered after the old 1662 Prayer Book. In fact I am inclined to believe that behind much perversity, such "conservatives" have something serious to say to the Church in their protest against pedestrian language in liturgy and the trivializing of faith. Their cry is for those deeper things which elude the grasp of theological formulae and which are carried to us through the carefully woven texture of symbol and ritual. However it was clear to me that most Catholics I met, like most Anglicans, were neither very conservative nor very radical, but somewhere in the sane middle. They wanted the Church to be the wise scribe bringing out of his treasure things new and old (Matthew 13:52), and they were secure enough in faith to welcome the opening of the doors to new experiences and yet not to be ashamed of valuing older customs.

I had in fact encountered impressive evidence of the Catholic Church's ability to assimilate ever more variety. At Barnard Castle we had hosted a Charismatic Day in our Parish Hall. It was not at all my scene, as guitarists playing gospel songs and exuding Christian happiness always plunge me into deep depression, but none the less I admired the way a Roman Catholic monk led the day and showed how this important area of religious experience could be at home within catholic unity and there given a balancing sacramentalism which it needed. Cardinal Suenens led a notable mission in the Univeristy of Oxford and managed to unite more Christians than I had ever seen united in that most sectarian of cities. The Cardinal was evidently both an evangelical and a catholic and this came across, not only in his nightly addresses in the Sheldonian Theatre but, for me, most movingly in the short homilies he preached at his daily Mass. Here was a blending of Word and Sacrament which spoke to all the diverse pieces of my religious background. On holiday in Austria we discovered the local parish church's ability to catch up into its liturgy both the splendours of Mozart on the Feast of the Assumption and, on a Sunday, a visiting American choir singing Negro Spirituals. To hear the words "Were you there when they crucified my Lord?" sung at the heart of the Eucharist, was to be given a fresh insight into how the evangelical Gospel is articulated in the sacrifice of the Mass. I am bound to say that I found this evidence of comprehensiveness poignant at a time when I had argued for the reservation of the Blessed Sacrament in St Mary's and, for the second time, had failed to convince the Parochial Church Council. It was a very untypical flight to Protestant negation which I think I only met again at St Mary's when I relayed the complaint of a French visitor that, in a church dedicated to Our Lady, there was no statue of her before which she could light a candle and say a prayer, and when I sensed the frisson of horror at the very thought of providing such a thing. I found these flashes of irrational prejudice amongst such reasonable and liberal people puzzling, and the fear of taking in a greater variety of religious expression a failure in comprehensiveness.

SEVEN

"In you we have found a home"

I had now reached the stage when I could not doubt that, were I a Martian coming to earth and trying to identify the middle of this curious stream of Christian life, I would head for the Church of Rome. I knew that there was no problem-free ecclesiastical area this side of the Heavenly Jerusalem, and that Rome was not all sweetness and light, but, considering the awful unnatural sin of schism between brothers and sisters in Christ, I could see no reason of substance for not being joined up to this old centre of unity. It really was no justification for continuing division to parade my English dislike of some of the alleged goings-on at the Vatican. I loved the Church of England but could see no reason for her continued separate existence, indeed I believed that her treasures found their natural home back in communion with Rome. She had had an honourable history and fed her children well, but she had always been something of a make-shift community, brought into existence by the confusion and strife of the English Reformation, and her wiser leaders had recognized this, teaching that the time would come when she would have to die in order to carry her treasure into a wider unity. I believed that the moment had come now, and that we dared not prevaricate and let it pass. Here were we Christians faced with issues which concerned the very future of the Gospel and we could simply no longer indulge in the luxury of division, wasting time dredging up all sorts of minor points to justify our separate existence. Our energy and devotion were needed for better things.

At this stage I realized what a gulf there is between

theory and practice. On the one side were heady notions and on the other the work in which I believed and the strong tug of my Anglican roots. I might have gone on for ever in this in-between world had I not been presented with an invitation to take up a new post. As I had served about eight years at St Mary's and the job offered was interesting, I gave it serious consideration. However, in advising me to accept, a senior bishop made the mistake of going on to outline the scenario of my future Anglican career as he saw it. It was an eerie feeling, to see myself so blatantly a pawn in a game of ecclesiastical chess, and although the prospect of what might lie ahead had a distinct appeal to the ambitious side of me, I came away from that interview depressed and feeling boxed in. As it became clear, for totally different reasons, that this post would not have been suitable, I had to recognize that sooner rather than later something else would be offered and I would face a crisis of integrity. Could I in all honesty accept further office in the Church of England? Through the generosity of my churchwardens and colleagues, I was offered a three-month sabbatical break. As this would be the first sustained break I had had in my ministry, I eagerly accepted the opportunity to stand back from things. They were three glorious months.

After a cold wet spring, the sun came out in June, and shone for the rest of the summer. The people of St Mary's were scrupulously careful to leave me alone, and I had the joy of sitting in our Oxford garden reading in a leasured way the first volume of Von Balthasar's *The Glory of the Lord*. I took the opportunity to make a private retreat at the Convent of the Incarnation, where the contemplative Sisters of the Love of God while managing both to preserve the integrity of their way of life generously share something of it with others. When you are played out, there is nothing like plugging into the life of a religious order and, instead of straining to revive yourself with all manner of piety, experience the community offering its praise and prayer, allowing yourself quietly to slip into its rhythm. It is a great way of rediscovering that prayer is first God's gift to us before ever it is our task.

The sabbatical ended with a family holiday in the Austrian mountains. The niggle had not gone away and, returning to our hotel after a long day's walk, I shared with James, my son, something of the dilemma. Both he and his sister are good listeners and I have always valued their advice. James was sympathetic, not simply because he appreciated the admirable brevity of Roman Catholic services, but also because he warmed to the international character of the Catholic Church and recognized the Pope's service of holding the show together. But his advice was typically astringent. He reckoned that I was suffering from "ministerial burnout", and counselled that I should stay with the Church of England and work for its unity with Rome.

The value of such a break is that you are forced to review what you have been doing, and disturbingly often the result is that you come to the conclusion that you ought to stop doing it. Standing back from the daily round I could see that the parish needed a new vicar who would bring a fresh and sharper mind to bear on its life. I ought to be looking for another job but could I do this with integrity? At last I was cornered; the old niggle had to be faced and a decision made once and for all as to whether this was an escapist illusion or some call from God.

But how does one distinguish between the voice of God and the lure of illusion? I have always been very suspicious of those "special guidances" which some claim to receive in their times of prayer. Of course in decision-making prayer matters a lot, and God does answer our prayers, yet, it has seemed to me that he answers them, not by shouting down the chimney in the time of prayer, but in the events and pressures which follow after our praying. What must be fostered in prayer is an alertness and sensitivity to what God may be saying through all the funny happenings of our daily life. My mother always found decisions very difficult, and in her later life, crippled by arthritis, could not decide whether to sell up her lovely but over-large house in Wiltshire. She always said she was waiting for a sign from God. However, when she broke a leg and it was suggested to her that this might be the requested sign, she judged, as we all do, that it was not quite clear enough. In the event the good Lord, knowing her agonies of indecision, let her off the hook and quietly took her to himself.

If I got no definite marching orders through my prayer, I was provided with a clue. Although God does not shout down the telephone to us, he does it seems sometimes haunt us with a particular passage of scripture, to which we find ourselves returning again and again, and which becomes invested with the power of a personal address. So I found these hard gospel words constantly popping up at me:

Whoever would save his life will lose it; and whoever loses his life for my sake and the gospel's will save it. For what does it profit a man to gain the whole world and forfeit his life? (Mark 8: 35 and 36).

I had an uncomfortable feeling that the next stage in my pilgrimage had to involve some piece of dying. There was nothing heroic or morbid about this but it was simply the only way to find happiness and fulfilment. These are difficult things to write about because words make it all sound more dramatic than it really was. Nor did the dying necessarily mean becoming a Roman Catholic. God provides for every one of us a bit of dying to be done, and each "death" is unique. Amongst my Anglican friends I had seen heroism of which I would not be capable – an academic giving up the studies he loved to take on all sorts of distasteful ecclesiastical administration, the country lover choosing to devote his life to ministry in the inner city. I knew that God had treated me very gently and had lavished a lot on me, but I suspected that he was now saying: "The time has come, lad, for a bit of handing back." Life did not stop still and there were lots of other things to occupy my mind, but as I prayed alone in St Mary's after Evensong or, at the end of each morning, exercised the dog by the river, my prayer was becoming increasingly simple: "God, I want to do your will, but I cannot unless you show me what it is!"

It was on one of these walks that I had an experience, which I gather is quite common, but which I have rarely had, that of being literally stopped in my tracks by an overwhelming sense of the sheer reality of God, of his being before me like a great solid mountain. It took my breath away and I saw, with a new sharpness, that nothing was more worthwhile than the "yes" I could make to God's will. However much a tangle of mixed motives I was, I had to grasp my freedom to respond to God. What was at issue was, not a rather boring matter of switching ecclesiastical allegiance, but taking the next step in my pilgrimage towards God.

But is this freedom simply an illusion? Every "convertion", whether from unbelief to belief, from one Church to another or even from one political party to another, can be explained away, the "convert" reduced to a victim of unconscious desires and pressures. We have all played this game with other people – the socialist friend who becomes a right wing monetarist, the disappointed businessman whose ambitions have not been realized who turns to religion and gets twice-born. How we pride ourselves on knowing more clearly than they do what has really motivated them! The sinister logic of this is followed out in the Soviet Union where dissidents are sometimes sent, not to prison, but to psychiatric hospitals. Dissent is treated as an illusion; the rebel is not wicked but mad.

So I reached a low point when a friend said something like this to me: "You are the same romantic who, as a teenager, became a conscientious objector and who, as a young priest, dissented from the majority opinion of the Church and State Commission. You like to be in the awkward squad, there to luxuriate in escape and ir-responsibility. If you want to do the really difficult thing, you will stay with the Church of England, endure its muddles and loose ends, and not opt for a quiet life in the bosom of Rome." These words left me wondering whether, apart from this bundle of mixed motives, there was anything of me left. If, after all these years of ponder-ing, I was nothing more than the victim of a conflict between ambition and escapism, what value was there in pretending to decide about anything? I was the pawn on the bishop's chessboard whose destiny it was, not to choose and decide, but to submit to being moved around. I had never felt so helpless and naked. Yet my friend's fiery darts could not be ignored. If I had to fight for my freedom, I could not do so by ignoring the tangle of my motives. I needed counsel and help from those who stood outside my situation.

I had already discovered that Ralph Townsend, by then Chaplain of Lincoln College, was agonizing over the same problem. It was a consolation to know that someone so sanely indifferent to ecclesiastical politics and so utterly lacking in solemnity about himself, should be in the same boat. But I needed as well more detached advice. That came from Gordon Wakefield, the Methodist Principal of Queen's College, Birmingham. Gordon had preached on several occasions at St Mary's and I had come to ap-preciate his wise and generous friendship. On a damp, sombre November day, we walked by the river and I told him all about my problem. He was sad but, as a deeply catholic Methodist, showed great sympathy with the issues which had concerned me.

Having discovered that one friend was not too shocked, I tried another, Mark Santer, the Bishop of Kensington. I had to be in London for what proved to be my swan song as a disestablishmentarian, to appear with Eric Heffer and Donald Reeves on the radio debate programme "You the Jury". Despite the more smoothly organized case of the establishment party, led by John Gummer, we managed, mainly through the swashbuckling good humour of Eric Heffer, to convert the audience to our point of view. Before going to Broadcasting House I saw Mark Santer, whose counsel, as always, was incisive. "Make no decision", he advised, "until you have done the Ignatian Exercises. This will provide you with the probing you need and, by putting yourself into the hands of an experienced conductor of the Exercises, you will be given an objective point of reference." This advice was as generous as it was good for Mark, as co-chairman of ARCIC 2, is committed to the cause of corporate unity, and his every instinct must have been to persuade me to stay put to help the cause along. Mark was one of many Anglican friends who provided me with space to make up my own mind. As a result of his advice, I put myself into the hands of an equally committed ecumenist, a Jesuit, to guide me through the Spiritual Exercises of St Ignatius Loyola.

If you were to sit down and read the Exercises you would not make much of them, for they read like a car-driving or a do-it-yourself handyman's guide. They are precisely what the title suggests, exercises, merely sketching out a task to be performed, and so they only come alive when they are worked on. Under the supervision of a director, the task is shaped to the needs of the individual and thus becomes a splendid practical expression of what used to be called "personal religion". In its businesslike and practical pursuit of holiness, I found all sorts of connections with the tradition of Methodist spirituality. Some are able to get away and do the Exercises in retreat conditions, but others have to use the opportunity to work through them amidst their ordinary commitments. For family and work reasons, I had to choose the latter. I do not regret this as the Exercises, done in the world, have their own value and make their own particular demands. You need to set aside an extra hour a day for prayer and make time to see your director once a week. The experience was exactly what I needed. The meditations set out by Ignatius are extremely visual, confronting us with a series of gospel pictures, and after all my attempts to think things through, it was good to be turned from ideas to the centre of it all, the person of our Lord. Before the crucified and risen Christ the heart is probed, and existing ties and obligations are faced. Gently you are eased out of the dream world of ideas and carefully led to the moment of decision. Instead of waiting around for some great divine illumination, the pros and cons of any proposed action have to be weighed, even to be written down as a sober shopping list. Yet in this commonsense exercise there is no suggestion of a Pelagian pulling of oneself up to heaven by one's own bootlaces, for it is held in the context of a trust that God will give what has been prayed for, that understanding of his will for which the heart has longed.

As truthfully as possible, I tried to face up to the dangers and benefits of remaining in the Church of England or becoming a Roman Catholic. To stay meant continuing to exercise a ministry in which I believed, and through which I had opportunities to be of service to people. In this ministry what gifts I had could be used. I would be able to do my bit for the cause of Christian unity and could go on working for a church with a firm heart and open arms. Despite the fact that I would have to seek a new job, this course would be less disruptive and traumatic for the family and I would be able to remain in solidarity with my friends, especially those who were on the front-line of the Church of England's tensions. By remaining an Anglican I would be reaffirming my roots – but would the Roman niggle really go away? It had stubbornly survived the move from Barnard Castle to Oxford, and I could see that its persistence was having a debilitating effect on my work. If I were to stand up for the things in which I believed, I would inevitably become involved in dreary controversy and I feared greatly becoming a grumbling and disloyal marginalized Anglican. Membership of a small group which held that it, and it alone, was the true Church of England, held no attractions for me. Such party sects seemed only a breeding ground for lopsidedness and eccentricity. If I was to go on swimming in the Anglican stream, it had to be in mid-stream, but it was there alas that the niggle continued.

So I turned to the advantages of becoming a Roman Catholic. I was convinced that here the Catholic Church subsisted, that this was the centre of the Christian thing. Need I really deny my precious roots by stepping forward into Catholic unity, for did I not believe that it was here that these gifts of my past really belonged? Yes, it would mean giving up the ministry I so loved, but perhaps that was what God wanted from me; not to hand back something I had ceased to believe in, but to hand back with gratitude and trust what had meant so much. I had come to see that there could be no unity without seeds falling into the ground to die. Perhaps my vocation was to do what we all, in some way or other, will have to do in the end. Of course there were dangers. It all sounded uncomfortably self-dramatizing and attention-seeking. No Vicar of St Mary's in Oxford could become a Roman Catholic without the shades of his illustrious predecessor, Newman, being invoked. Was this not a subtle way of getting the best of both worlds, making a bit of a splash while heading for the joys of escape, a fiendishly clever piece of self-indulgence and irresponsibility? What about my family, whose very faith could be disturbed by such a disruption, and what about my friends, especially those who were feeling ground down by the politics of the Church of England? Where was the love in all this, where the opportunities to move out from myself to be of service to others?

The moment for decision came, and when it did I knew, as clearly as I have ever known anything, what I had to do. At least I had to conclude that if, after this tedious huffing and puffing, I had not made the right decision, then the chances of ever doing so again were pretty remote. I found myself jotting down this conclusion:

During the past few months, God has led me to see that all this goes deeper than a change of ecclesiastical allegiance. It has to do with my personal pilgrimage into faith, with my own further convertion to him. In this I have been called to a greater love and gratitude for my roots, so that I see more clearly what I have been given in my Anglican past, but I have also heard the call to go forward to discover that the path of creativity has to involve a handing back to God, not angrily or contemptuously rejecting what has been given, but saying "This is what you have made me. This is what you have done through me. Now I must believe you enough to hand it back. Going forward into Catholic Unity is simply the way of doing what, for me, is your will." It is all very painful and there are great areas of loss and depression yet to be faced. Sometimes all I can do is say: "If it is true, then I must do it." But occasionally a bit of resurrection light gets through and I have a deep-down feeling that "all things are well, all manner of things are well".

*

The mechanics of disengagement proved more complex than I had imagined. I had discussed the matter, not only with close friends, but with the churchwardens of St Mary's and a few elder statesmen in the congregation. There was something of a conflict between the desire to minimize damage to the Church of England and the need to treat the congregation in a pastorally responsible way. The former, it was judged, would be best served by a departure speedy to the point of abruptness, while the latter needed a gentler process with some opportunity to explain what I was doing. The Bishop of Oxford, whom I had consulted at an early stage, overcame his obvious distress, and provided loving support as I tried to work out a programme which would do justice to both interests. In the end there was a compromise which, I suppose, proved unsatisfactory to all.

On 19 May, my fifty-first birthday, I concelebrated the Eucharist with my colleagues and at the end of the service, read a brief but carefully prepared statement (see Appendix). My final sermon was at Evensong when I preached on "The Re-union of Friends". The Newman shadow had to be faced but while my predecessor had preached his last sermon on "The Parting of Friends" in the sad autumn of the year, I was able to preach in the spring, the season of hope and new growth. We all longed for the re-union of friends, that unity for which our Lord had prayed, and although there were still real hurts and partings, yet there were evident signs that the Holy Spirit of convergence was at work.

It was a pretty grim birthday, not made any better by the thought that, had I continued a few weeks longer, I could have celebrated the twenty-fifth anniversary of my ordination as priest in York Minster. But there was light in the darkness. Chris and Julia Foster carried us off for a wonderful birthday lunch, encapsulating in their hospitality all the generous support they had given us over those last difficult months. And there was further light in the loving and sensitive reaction of the people of St Mary's. Sad and bewildered though they were, they never gave the impression that this had to mean the parting of friends. Their Christian maturity was sorely tested and I was proud that they had come through with flying colours. John Henry Newman must have looked somewhat wistfully at the farewell party and gifts we were given on our departure. Things had moved on since his days, and the forces of convergence were proving stronger than those of divergence.

Inevitably there was a mild flurry of publicity, and for forty-eight hours the telephone rang rather more than usual, and I got used to reading out my statement and telling reporters that I had nothing further to say. As the *Daily Telegraph* correspondent had been in the congregation on 19 May and had produced a full and accurate report, the story was able to die its natural death rather earlier than it might have done. Media exposure follows the law of my old Irish uncle's favourite text: "It came to pass." The publicity did however elicit a shoal of letters containing a variety of comment and advice. There were only three angry letters, sadly all from Anglican friends, but only a little less painful were the smattering of triumphalist Catholic letters in which trumpets were blown rather noisily as one soul passed from the darkness of error into the light of the true faith. Clearly there were some Catholics who, despite the clear teaching of Vatican 2, believed that there was no genuine Christian experience outside the walls of Rome. Some were so extreme that they felt bound to warn me of the dangers of entering the post-conciliar Church. I might be jumping out of the frying-pan into the fire, for the Catholic Church, I was told, had been infiltrated by Masons, Socialists and Liberals. However, most of the letters, whether from Anglicans or Roman Catholics, were not like that, but sane, loving and supportive. Perhaps the one I valued most came from a Catholic prison chaplain who had got his flock praying for all the family. Indeed this was one of those occasions when you feel almost physically held up and kept going by the prayers of others.

On the next two Sundays we worshipped together as a family in St Mary's, for although my public ministry had ended, I felt free for a while to remain in a lay capacity as a friend amongst friends. There were, in any case, many administrative loose ends to be tied up, and the Bishop had been extraordinarily kind about our staying on in the vicarage until the end of the children's school term. It was on 12 July, at a Mass for Christian unity at the Catholic Chaplaincy, that I was received into the full unity of the Catholic Church. Rod Strange, the Catholic chaplain, conducted the whole thing with great ecumenical sensitivity, and although by then I was drained of almost any religious feeling, I found it a moving occasion, for without implying any rejection of my past, it expressed simply and clearly all that was positive in the step I was taking.

And so on 25 July, having disposed of or stored some of our accumulated possessions, we left Oxford to start a new life in the village of Hailey outside Witney. We were fortunate in owning a two-bedroom cottage to retreat to and having sufficient resources to keep us going for a year or so. It has meant that the family could have a period of some stability and that there has been no immediate pressure on me to find a new job. So I have a bit of space to discover where the "Leading Light" would take me next.

It is good to settle into the life of a rural Catholic parish, and amazing to feel how much one has come home. I have particularly appreciated the strong sense of solidarity in a common faith which exists amongst Catholics. Instead of straining to forge a faith of one's own it is a relief to seek simply to share the faith of one's brothers and sisters. Before Christmas I went, as I always did as an Anglican, to make my confession, but this year there was a difference; I went not as a lone individual to do something which, in the Church of England, is looked upon as eccentric or an act of exceptional piety, but in a queue of penitents doing what was ordinary and natural. There was nothing exceptional about us; we were all just sinners lining up again to hear the words of our Saviour's forgiveness. This does not mean that I find myself relaxing into the cosy security of a feather bed. Familiar problems and tensions, which I had known in an Anglican setting, are here to greet me as old friends, for in truth they know no denominational barriers. So I meet radicals who want to press forwards and conservatives who want to put things into reverse, but I find myself rather unexcited about a conflict which the media seem to dramatize and distort. The priority remains what I was taught as a child it should be – to become more Christ-like and, in working out what this means for individuals and institutions, I guess that neither a radical Boff nor a conservative Ratzinger has a monopoly of insight.

If it is good to settle in as a backbench Catholic, it is also good through my family to have those Anglican roots kept alive. Before going to Mass every Sunday I worship with them at the local parish church. My wife and children gave me the freedom to make my own decision and have bravely shouldered a lot of the consequences. It is important now that I should make space for them to make their own conscientious decisions. It is an experience more terrible than I had realized to be divided at the altar rails, and the so easily mouthed slogan about "the pain of our unhappy divisions" has come alive to us with a vengeance, but I am grateful for this continuing Anglican experience which accentuates my longing that this precious piece of Christian life should, in its integrity and uniqueness, find its home again in Catholic unity.

There are other pains. You cannot do a job for twenty-five years and give it up without a sense of loss. At times I am overcome with a sense of vertigo when suddenly what I have done becomes sharply real. I have dreams of being at the altar in St Mary's or going about my old pastoral work, and then I awake – and I confess that it is with tears. I even have twinges of nostalgia for those P.C.C. meetings I used to dread! Like others who are unemployed I have to cope with the loss of that structure imposed from without which, with its chores, may have seemed so irritating and yet which holds us together. As I mourn the loss of being useful, I discover how dependent I have become on being needed and so perceive how possessive this care for others has often been.

I think that I begin to see that, in being stripped of role and function to plain Peter Raphael, God still has some lessons to teach me. I remember a saintly Anglican bishop whose life centred on his daily celebration of the Eucharist. The time came when old age and sickness made this impossible, and his friends thought what a terrible blow this would be. In fact he took it all calmly, simply handing this precious gift back to God and entering into a deeper level of priesthood, where all he had to offer was himself in his weakness and diminishment. Every priest must one day endure this loss of role and function, for every priest must die and know that his priesthood will then be focused in those words, "Father into they hands I commend my spirit".

I was already beginning to wrestle with the consequences of my impending decision when, for the last time, I preached the Three Hour Devotion at St Mary's on Good Friday. I was haunted by that poem of R. S. Thomas, "The Porch". Of the priest he says:

He was like
Anyone else, a man with
ears and eyes.

He has no power to pray. He is found, not in the sanctuary, but in the porch with his back turned on the interior. Half in and half out, he is the true priest just because he has eyes and ears and looks out on a universe. Although with no power to pray, he is driven to his knees and "he keeps his place there for one hour on that lean threshold". In this I begin to see the face of Jesus our great High Priest. The Epistle to the Hebrews is full of sacred images, of priesthood, temple, sanctuary and the apparatus of worship, but all these images are taken and applied to the shocking secular reality of Jesus hanging on the Cross outside the city walls. He is a man like anyone else, "made like his brethren in every respect", and he is the priest because with eyes of compassion he looks out on a universe and with ears hears its cry of pain. Here in deepest solidarity with us he is wholly and completely for God. Not in a cultic act, but in his living and dying he becomes the "one full perfect and sufficient sacrifice", never more so than in the passivity of being stripped and hanging in weakness and death. I think that I begin to glimpse that it is not so much a matter of giving up priesthood as of learning to enter into it more deeply. After all, priest-wise the most important day in my life was not ordination in 1960 but my baptism in 1934. Before the call to a particular ministerial priesthood had come the earlier call to be a member of the royal priesthood of the people of God. Maybe God is providing me with an opportunity to rediscover and reclaim my share in that priesthood. The sense of loss remains but I am saved from too much self-pity by the recognition that there are many others in the same boat as myself, not only priests who, through sickness, have had to give up active ministry, but Free Church ministers who have become Anglicans, Catholic priests who have become married, and perhaps most poignant of all those women, who believing themselves called to be priests, cannot even have their calling tested. There is a growing underground of frustrated priesthood and I have some feeling of solidarity with it.

It is a sad fact that the ecumenist who jumps the gun, whether as an Anglican becoming a Roman Catholic or a Methodist becoming an Anglican, finds himself an embarrassment to those who are labouring for corporate unity. Matters are not improved by the sort of Roman Catholic triumphalist who hails such transitions as evidence that if the Catholic Church sticks to her guns, the ripe fruits of discontented Anglicans will drop into her lap, so confirming his belief that there is no other reunion but this. I find this a tragic misreading of the situation. Indeed the Church has to manifest an element of intransigence but this should be, not the intransigence of institutional pride, but that of the Gospel, of the God who stands before us as the great Rock. The Church has the privilege of carrying this treasure but, where she is consumed by institutional pride, the treasure is hidden and the unsearchable riches of Christ are invested with all the attractions of a time-bomb. It was the faithful implementation of Vatican 2 which allowed me to see behind some very unattractive legalism and ecumenical insensitivity to the face of Christ himself. I am not pretending that the post-conciliar Church is some brand new Church which has at last become attractive to the children of the Reformation; the continuities with the past are just as obvious as the changes. What I do claim, with all the energy at my command, is that because it involved not just modernization but genuine Gospel renewal, Vatican 2 has revealed more clearly the unsearchable riches of Christ. Nothing drew me more strongly into Catholic unity than the renewed vision of a Church firm at the centre and boldly opening out into a world seen, not just as the realm of sin and darkness, but still marked by the sign of a loving Creator. Nothing drew me more strongly than an affirmation of Catholic unity and fullness which was able joyfully to affirm the rich experience of other Christian communities. I grant that this is a much less neat and secure way of presenting the Gospel than that of the sole fortress of light confronting a world of darkness, but I do not see the Lord of the Church having much time for those who wrap up the Gospel treasure to hide it in the security of the earth.

I wonder how the ecumenical pilgrimage will turn out in practice, just what, if the forces of convergence are triumphant and agreed statements are accepted, will actually happen. I confess that I am haunted by the fact that history records many brave attempts to unite Christians and many sad failures to bring these attempts to fruition. Unity is much harder to achieve than disunity and, as we move tantalizingly near to the goal of our labours, we should be alert to the redoubled activity of the devil to frustrate our hopes. Indeed it seems possible for the hesitating and over-cautious, those who would wait until every "i" is dotted and every "t" crossed, every blemish removed from the beloved's face, simply to miss the boat. God's moment comes and we fail to grasp it. Might it not be that, without pretending to a role of undue importance, we who have been indecently impatient could sharpen this sense of urgency? Convergence is good but not quite enough. We shall not be able to be carried effortlessly on the waves of convergence into unity. Decision, commitment to one another and a willingness to die to separation will be needed. The day will come when God will challenge us to accept one another warts and all and, at last, take the plunge. For individuals it is hard enough but for institutions, with their built-in instinct for self-preservation, it is well nigh impossible. Yet with God all things are possible.

But if we, who believe that we have journeyed into a wider unity, are to be acceptable as goads and not dismissed as ecumenically irrelevant, then we shall have clearly to be those who value their roots and are able to carry into this wider unity that past experience. Friends most deeply involved in the life of the Church of England inevitably see what I have done as a betrayal and rejection of the Church they love. However much I may claim that I deny nothing of my past, however often I call myself an Anglican Roman Catholic, the breaking of fellowship and communion speaks more loudly than my words. To these friends I must frankly say that, for there to be Christian unity, all must become Roman Catholics. Yet to my Roman Catholic friends I must equally frankly say that, for there to be Christian unity, it must be possible for us to become Anglican, Methodist, Quaker and Presbyterian Roman Catholics. It has to be made evident that in journeying forward no riches have been lost. That constitutes for the Roman Catholic Church a continuing challenge to become yet more catholic, to make the room as broad and accepting of the various traditions as that called for by the Council. The Roman Communion has to show that it really is the city of which all can say "In you we have found a home".

Appendix

The following is the statement made to the congregation of the University Church of St Mary the Virgin, Oxford on Sunday 19 May 1985

*

I am about to resign as Vicar of St Mary's to seek admission to the Roman Catholic Church. This has been a difficult decision to make and I have been much helped by the loving support of my wife and family, the understanding of the Bishop of Oxford and the counsel of friends from many churches. At no point have they put me under pressure. They have been content to encourage me to probe the tangled web of my motives and seek what seems the will of God for me.

This is no sudden decision but a facing up to a niggle which has lasted for fourteen years. The reasons for my decision are inevitably complex but, at the heart of it, lies a growing conviction that the Christian enterprise is not a book or a club for religious do-it-yourself enthusiasts but a movement, a stream of life passing through different ages and cultures. In mid-stream are those Christians in communion with the Bishop of Rome. That stream has encountered log-jams of rubbish, the product of human sin and inertia. So I can understand frustrated reformers who have felt compelled to divert from the main stream. Yet I have come to see that such separation is ultimately destructive and diminishing. Christian creativity lies in unity. Variety is the spice of Christian life but this variety

138

must be held together in a coherent fellowship. We need one another's gifts to be balanced followers of Christ. For Christian unity I have always longed and prayed, a unity which is more like marriage than simply the friendly relations of good neighbours, a unity with bonds tough enough to hold together the lively treasures of Christian life. I continue to pray for that corporate unity for which the members of the Anglican-Roman Catholic International Commission labour with such patience and courage. I believe that those prayers will be answered. But, for my part, I can no longer see any reason of substance and principle to hold apart from the main-stream. Life is too short, the Gospel too precious, the human issues too serious to waste time thinking up reasons for preserving division.

Of course belonging to the stream of Christian life matters, not because it is cosier that way, but because this stream bears to us the Good News of Christ. As it moves through different ages and cultures, a developing understanding of the riches of Christ is required. This treasure is not for hiding safely in a hole. So I have loved the gentle generosity and scholarly freedom of the Church of England. Yet the Gospel is not unearthed by the labour of scholars, it is a gift revealed by God himself. The ministry of theological exploration needs to be complemented by a continuing ministry of affirmation. Human words are fragile and incomplete but I have come to see that the Church must be able to nail its colours to the mast, articulate the Gospel in the confidence that these earthen vessels can be carriers of the very Word of God.

My action will be seen as a bolt for safety and peace. I do not see it that way. There is in truth no escape from the problems or from human sin and ecclesiastical imperfection. Holding together variety and unity, authority and freedom is a humanly impossible task and we are tempted to give up and opt for one-sidedness. The Vatican, like

Parochial Church Councils and Synods, is all too human. But it is no use waiting around for the perfection of the Kingdom. We have to use what God has provided for us despite the fact that we have messed up his gifts. A point comes on the road to unity when, thanking God for all he has given us in our divided state, we have to take a risk deciding to go forward believing that, although the seed must fall into the ground and die, God can be trusted to produce a rich crop.

Over the last four months of careful thought and prayer, my Anglican roots have become more precious to me than ever. All that God has shown me of his truth I believe and will go on believing. But the point has come when God seems to be saying: "That risk you must now take by putting your life where your mouth is." What may look from the outside a rather boring and irrelevant change of ecclesiastical allegiance, has become for me a matter of going forward on the next stage of my personal pilgrimage. This I do with great apprehension and without in any way calling in question the integrity of others who must tread the path which God has allotted to them. Like John Henry Newman, "if I am obliged to bring religion into after-dinner toasts, I shall drink – to the Pope, if you please – still to Conscience first, and to the Pope afterwards." There is pain in all this, pain for myself in laying aside the ministry which I have loved over the past twenty-six years, and pain for others affected by my decision. The pain is inescapable and yet I believe that, if we focus on these matters of integrity and conscience, we shall avoid damaging one another and may even, God willing, discover a bit of Easter creativity.

Peter Cornwell
Vicar of the University Church
of St Mary the Virgin, Oxford

Also available in Fount Paperbacks

Journey for a Soul
GEORGE APPLETON

'Wherever you turn in this inexpensive but extraordinarily valuable paperback you will benefit from sharing this man's pilgrimage of the soul.'

Methodist Recorder

The Imitation of Christ
THOMAS A KEMPIS

After the Bible, this is perhaps the most widely read book in the world. It describes the way of the follower of Christ – an intensely practical book, which faces the temptations and difficulties of daily life, but also describes the joys and helps which are found on the way.

Autobiography of a Saint: Thérèse of Lisieux
RONALD KNOX

'Ronald Knox has bequeathed us a wholly lucid, natural and enchanting version . . . the actual process of translating seems to have vanished, and a miracle wrought, as though St Teresa were speaking to us in English . . . his triumphant gift to posterity.'

G. B. Stern, The Sunday Times

The Way of a Disciple
GEORGE APPLETON

'. . . a lovely book and an immensely rewarding one . . . his prayers have proved of help to many.'

Donald Coggan

Also available in Fount Paperbacks

The Sacrament of the Present Moment
JEAN-PIERRE DE CAUSSADE

'It is good to have this classic from the days of the Quietist tensions with its thesis that we can and must find God in the totality of our immediate situation . . .'

The Expository Times

The Poems of St John of the Cross
TRANSLATED BY ROY CAMPBELL

'Mr Campbell has recreated the extraordinary subtlety of the music of the original in an English verse worthy of it and that climbs from aspiration to ecstasy as if it were itself the poem.'

The Guardian

Thérèse of Lisieux
MICHAEL HOLLINGS

A superb portrait of one of the most popular of all saints.

'This book is well worth recommending . . . presents a simple factual outline of Thérèse's life and teaching . . . (with) incidents . . . applied to our own everyday lives.'

Review for Contemplatives of all Traditions

I, Francis
CARLO CARRETTO

This unusual and compelling book is a sustained meditation on the spirituality of St Francis of Assisi, bringing the meaning of his message to our time.

'A book one will not forget.'

Eric Doyle, The Tablet

Also available in Fount Paperbacks

Fount Paperbacks

Fount is one of the leading paperback publishers of religious books and below are some of its recent titles.

- [ ] THE WAY OF ST FRANCIS Murray Bodo £2.50
- [ ] GATEWAY TO HOPE Maria Boulding £1.95
- [ ] LET PEACE DISTURB YOU Michael Buckley £1.95
- [ ] DEAR GOD, MOST OF THE TIME YOU'RE QUITE NICE Maggie Durran £1.95
- [ ] CHRISTIAN ENGLAND VOL 3 David L Edwards £4.95
- [ ] A DAZZLING DARKNESS Patrick Grant £3.95
- [ ] PRAYER AND THE PURSUIT OF HAPPINESS Richard Harries £1.95
- [ ] THE WAY OF THE CROSS Richard Holloway £1.95
- [ ] THE WOUNDED STAG William Johnston £2.50
- [ ] YES, LORD I BELIEVE Edmund Jones £1.75
- [ ] THE WORDS OF MARTIN LUTHER KING Coretta Scott King (Ed) £1.75
- [ ] BOXEN C S Lewis £4.95
- [ ] THE CASE AGAINST GOD Gerald Priestland £2.75
- [ ] A MARTYR FOR THE TRUTH Grazyna Sikorska £1.95
- [ ] PRAYERS IN LARGE PRINT Rita Snowden £2.50
- [ ] AN IMPOSSIBLE GOD Frank Topping £1.95
- [ ] WATER INTO WINE Stephen Verney £2.50

All Fount paperbacks are available at your bookshop or newsagent, or they can be ordered by post from Fount Paperbacks, Cash Sales Department, G.P.O. Box 29, Douglas, Isle of Man, British Isles. Please send purchase price, plus 15p per book, maximum postage £3. Customers outside the U.K. send purchase price, plus 15p per book. Cheque, postal or money order. No currency.

NAME (Block letters) _____

ADDRESS _____

_____